Autistic Spectrum Di

The SEN series

Able, Gifted and Talented – Janet Bates and
  Sarah Munday
Dyspraxia – Geoff Brookes
Profound and Multiple Learning Difficulties –
  Corinna Cartwright and Sarah Wind-Cowie
ADHD – Fintan O'Regan
*Surviving and Succeeding in Special Educational
  Needs* – Fintan O'Regan
Visual Needs – Olga Miller and Adam Ockelford
Language and Communication Difficulties –
  Dimitra Hartas
Dyslexia – Gavin Reid
Emotional and Behavioural Difficulties – Roy Howarth
  and Pam Fisher
Autistic Spectrum Disorders – Sarah Worth

Autistic Spectrum Disorders

Sarah Worth

continuum
LONDON • NEW YORK

Continuum International Publishing Group

The Tower Building   15 East 26th Street
11 York Road   New York, NY 10010
London
SE1 7NX

www.continuumbooks.com

British Library Cataloguing-in-Publication Data
A catalogue record for this book is available from the British Library.

ISBN: 0–8264–7994–4 (paperback)

Typeset by Servis Filmsetting Ltd, Manchester
Printed and bound in Great Britain by MPG Books Ltd, Bodmin,
Cornwall

Contents

1

Autistic Spectrum Disorders

The Triad of Impairments

Autism has affected people throughout history (see
www.myautis.com/famousaspies.html) and occurs in
all countries and cultures of the world. In 1943 a physi-
cian named Leo Kanner published a description of a
group of children with the following characteristics:

♦ an extreme aloneness and lack of social res-
  ponsiveness;

♦ an obsessive desire for the preservation of sameness;

♦ an excellent rote memory;

♦ mutism, or delayed language development including
  echolalia (i.e. echoing what has been said without
  understanding);

♦ an oversensitivity to sensory stimuli;

♦ a tendency toward repetitive activities and play.

And, as if society had signalled its readiness to recognize these difficulties, in 1944 Hans Asperger quite
independently published his findings about children

with similar problems, although his observations included some differences:

♦ motor clumsiness and lack of coordination;
♦ relatively normal language development and abilities.

It does appear that, in their joint discovery of what they both referred to as 'autistic' syndromes (from *autos*, meaning 'self'), Kanner and Asperger were describing different aspects of a similar condition. Today, people identified with the classic, or Kanner's, type of autism are more likely to be aloof, lack play, language and communication skills and be rigidly resistant to change. In contrast, people who are thought to have Asperger's syndrome tend to experience the same need and desire as most other people for social contact, but find it difficult to form social relationships and have little apparent *language* difficulty but do have difficulty *communicating*. They also usually have an interest in narrowly focused repetitive pastimes.

Since the 1940s, many researchers and professionals in the field of autism have attempted to find ways of diagnosing the condition. Diagnostic criteria for autism were first included in the *International Classification of Diseases* in 1978, and it is still deemed to be a medical diagnosis. By 1996, Dr Lorna Wing, having conducted research to establish whether there were indeed difficulties common to all children with autism, formulated the idea of an **autistic spectrum**: in other words, autism cannot be seen as a 'pure' or simply defined condition. Across the spectrum, individuals with autism will be as different from each other as they are from members of the general population; but they will all have the same types of well-defined difficulties. These are now known as the **Triad of Impairments**.

1. Impairments of social interaction: varying in difficulty from being aloof and wishing to remain isolated to interacting with others inappropriately and presenting as socially awkward and gauche; a limited understanding of the two-way nature of relationships.

2. Impairments of social language and communication: varying from the failure of language to develop, through to the tendency to say a lot without understanding the subtleties of language (e.g. jokes, metaphor); difficulty understanding non-verbal communication.

3. Impairments of flexibility of thought and imagination: a preference for ritualistic and repetitive types of activity and play; a marked resistance to change and difficulty generalizing skills or knowledge.

In addition to these three areas, it is believed – particularly by people who themselves have autism – that there is a fourth area of impairment.

4. Impairments of sensory processing and motor skills: differences in the way that sensory information (including pain) is experienced and a tendency to clumsiness and lack of coordination, particularly in the use of fine motor skills.

A diagnosis of **autistic spectrum disorder** (ASD), as it is now known, must encompass the identification of difficulties in each of these areas. ASD is:

◆ pervasive, i.e. affecting all aspects of a person's life;

◆ developmental, i.e. begins in infancy (with problems being present before the age of 3 years) and affects all areas of development;

◆ life-long.

It is not appropriate to think of ASD in terms of a 'cure': instead, it is a matter of enabling people with ASD to achieve their maximum potential in what amounts to a 'foreign' world. The causes of ASD are not fully understood at present, although research is continuing and some of those research areas are looked at in the sections on the psychological and biological theories later in this chapter.

Case studies

The following three (fictional) case studies, of quite different children, may help to clarify the distinctive characteristics of ASD. The first child, Hannah, has the type of ASD known as classic, or Kanner's, autism; the second and third children, Daniel and James, have Asperger's syndrome.

Case study 1: Hannah

Hannah was born following a normal pregnancy, and initially her first year of infancy appeared to be unremarkable. As she began walking, so her interest in her environment and the people in it diminished, and she stopped using the few words she had acquired (e.g. 'Mum', 'drink'). Her favourite plaything at this time was the small metal ring securing the strap on a bag of her mother's, which she twiddled with for long periods of time. She took the bag with her everywhere, even to bed, and was inconsolable without it; but if it was lost she simply stood and screamed until it was recovered. She was also attracted to running water, loved watching patterns of light on the floor, and would happily stand watching the washing machine revolve. She was inexplicably terrified of the newspaper and the post being put through the letterbox.

By the time Hannah was 5 years old, family life had become very stressful, as Hannah was increasingly frustrated and destructive, and all trips out were abandoned. She showed little preference for any one person in particular, and if she wanted anything she would merely take and direct people's hands in the general direction of the desired object. She occasionally said words (e.g. lawnmower) but did not use them meaningfully and they were seldom repeated. She reacted strongly if anyone moved her possessions, and was distressed by any change, even, for example, if her mother changed her hairstyle. Her diet was extremely restricted and she ate only cornflakes without milk and cream crackers with no margarine; she preferred particular brands (testing by smelling them) and refused to eat other brands. An attractive child, with an intelligent expression, she was physically strong and agile; her parents had been forced to place bars at her bedroom window to prevent her climbing out, as she was oblivious to the dangers of doing so.

Case study 2: Daniel

Daniel reached all his developmental milestones at the normal times, although he did seem to be quite a bit clumsier than his siblings and found it particularly difficult learning how to ride a tricycle. His mother was very proud that, at 2.5 years old, he knew not only all his colours, but his numbers and letter names too. At his 3-year check his Health Visitor was impressed, but also slightly disquieted, by his use of the word 'penultimate'. Daniel was passionate about Thomas the Tank Engine, and collected everything to do with it. He would play the same part of 'Thomas' videos over and over again, and could repeat chunks of the narrative. He also liked watching advertisements and, on seeing his grandmother coming down the street one day, he ran delightedly up to her and announced, 'Bold washes brighter!'

When Daniel started playschool, he appeared to be overwhelmed by the noise and activity of the other children, and although he sometimes watched them from the edge of the room, he made few attempts to speak to them. If someone came to join him as he was playing with the train track, he usually walked away. He enjoyed adult company, however, and loved to sit on the assistant's knee and tell her about entire episodes of 'Thomas'. He could attend for long periods to things that interested him, but only for a very short time to work set by the teacher.

When Daniel started school it became evident that he could read, but that he found it very difficult to follow a story or think about the characters' actions. He preferred books containing facts, and his interest changed from 'Thomas' to sharks, which he talked about even when people weren't listening. He found it difficult to sit with the rest of the group on the carpet, and he seemed to believe that the teacher was talking only to him – so he was puzzled to be told off for interrupting. In the playground one day he hit another child, and when asked why, he explained that he was only hitting back. In fact, the other child had tapped his arm to ask if he wished to join their game.

Case study 3: James

James enjoyed primary school and made good progress academically. He had been part of a small group of friends and, although he was viewed by both staff and children as a bit eccentric, he was accepted just as he was. At home, he was felt to be very like his uncle and grandfather and his family were not particularly concerned as he made the move to secondary school.

However, once there his behaviour (odd gait, loud voice and use of 'long' words, forthright opinions) soon made him the target of bullies and the group of friends – mindful of their own status – melted away. He found it very difficult to organize himself, never seemed to have the right equipment or be in the right place, and his attempts to explain himself were interpreted as rudeness and arrogance.

James continued to cope in most lessons, and particularly enjoyed science and IT. But break times were difficult for him and he generally went to the library to get away from the other students, including the bullies. However, one pupil from his last school gave James the impression that he was offering friendship and included him in some of their activities. In his pleasure at being part of a group again James allowed himself to be 'set-up' by the other pupils and, thinking that they were all sharing a joke, he was involved in a serious incident in which a Year 7 girl was indecently assaulted.

When it was eventually established what had actually happened James was vindicated, but became more socially isolated than ever. His schoolwork started to deteriorate and he began to experience a good deal of anxiety and depression.

How many people have autistic spectrum disorder?

The most recent and reliable studies, using the criteria of the standard diagnostic handbooks, are showing a prevalence of around 60 per 10,000 for autistic spectrum disorders with an estimate of between 8 and 30 per 10,000 for autism in its more classic *[i.e. Kanner's type]* form.

(from: Uta Frith, *Autism: Explaining the Enigma*, 2003, p. 59)

These figures have significant implications for all schools: on average, a primary school of a moderate size might have one to two children with ASD, while a high school of 1,000 pupils may have up to six children with ASD. Most of these pupils will be boys: four out of every five people with ASD are male, rising to 19 out of every 20 people with Asperger's syndrome.

What is autistic spectrum disorder?

The psychological theories

It is helpful, when trying to understand how having autism affects people, to consider the processes underlying their view of the world. Several theories about the way we, and people with autism, think have been developed. None of them are, on their own, complete explanations, but together they help to convey the concept of ASD.

The theory of mind mechanism

This approach has its roots in evolutionary theory. The early human mind that could make assumptions about other people's thoughts and intentions was more likely to survive and succeed in an unforgiving and competitive world. There are three elements.

1. The detection of motion and intention.

2. The ability to determine the direction someone's eyes are looking in.

3. Shared or joint attention to the same object.

These three elements combine to make the fourth, known as the 'theory of mind mechanism'. In more everyday terms, this is the ability most of us have to 'mind-read' the thoughts, motives and intentions of others; to work out what they are thinking – the very essence of all soap operas!

Although difficulties in this respect are not confined to people with ASD, their ability to 'read' other people is usually impaired to varying degrees. The following version of a much-repeated test given to children with ASD will help to illustrate this.

Activity 1

Imagine that I have placed my watch on the desk. I just want to nip to the next room to get something. I don't want Sophie taking my watch while I'm gone, so I quickly slip it under the book I was reading. Sophie sees me do this, however, and she sneaks in, takes the watch from under the book and puts it in the box of paper clips. And out she goes.

Q. When I come back (and this is NOT a catch question!), where will I **look** for my watch?

Under the book, of course! And when researchers asked a group of normally developing 4 year olds, that's what most of them said. So did most of a group of children with Down's syndrome, who had a mental age equivalent of 4 years. But when a group of children with ASD (with the same cognitive ability) were asked, most said that I would look in the box of paper clips.

There are at least two things going on here:

1. People with ASD tend to think visually, so their idea of where I would look for the watch is dominated by the visual actuality of the situation.

2. This is the problem with not knowing about other people's thoughts: that I might *believe* something that is, in fact, wrong, is very hard for people with ASD to understand. They may be able to learn how to analyse these sorts of conundrums – but they

have to make a conscious effort to learn, they don't understand intuitively as other people might do.

Incidentally, they usually don't enjoy soap operas, either!

The theory of interpersonal relatedness
Researchers, including Peter Hobson (2002), have suggested that infants and children usually develop an awareness of other people through the experience of relationships between people, beginning – in most cases – with mother and baby. This type of awareness is thought to be an innate capacity, allowing babies to gradually become conscious of their own thoughts and feelings, leading to an eventual awareness of others' thoughts and feelings.

Hobson suggests that in ASD self-awareness and self-concept are limited, so there is a failure to develop an understanding or awareness of a sense of 'other' in relation to the people around them. This is highlighted by their difficulties with the social sense inherent in the use of the personal pronouns, 'you' and 'I'. They might say, for example, 'do you want a drink?' meaning, 'I want a drink'.

Activity 2
Look at these two passages written by two 10 year olds when asked to describe themselves. What are the main differences between them?

I am a girl. I have long brown hair and blue eyes. I go to Park Fields School. My best friend is called Jessica. I have one brother called Luke and a sister called Emily. My mum works in a bank and my dad works at the hospital. I like going swimming with my friends and reading Harry Potter.

I am a boy. I go to Park Fields School and I am in Year 6. I have brown hair and browny kind of eyes. I like playing on the computer and I am good at Play Station games. I collect dinosaur models. I am learning to play chess.

The girl's passage is not just about her, she has already learned to define herself in relation to the people in her world. In contrast, the boy's passage is all about himself and his own interests; he does not include anyone else in his self-definition. This in itself is not, of course, diagnostic; but the failure to relate successfully to others is a necessary factor in making a diagnosis of ASD.

The theory of executive function
This approach originated from investigations into brain function and the possibility that ASD is the result of problems in the frontal lobes. These are the areas of the cerebral cortex responsible for the integration of many other functions: thinking, organizing, planning; and they also play a major role in the interpretation and control of the emotions. It is thought that consciousness and self-awareness (a sense of 'I') is centred in the frontal lobes.
Researchers have identified difficulties for people with ASD in:

♦ planning and organizing actions and responses;

♦ generalizing skills and learning;

♦ adapting to change;

♦ a tendency to perseverate (carry on doing or saying something repetitively);

♦ controlling impulses;

♦ multi-tasking.

Temple Grandin (1995, p. 145), in writing about her own autism, says:

> [I] cannot hold one piece of information in my mind while I manipulate the next step in the sequence.

To give one example: people with ASD, who are skilled mathematicians, are able to manipulate numbers in complex ways that are mysterious to most of us; but they may nevertheless appear to lack common sense and have great difficulty *applying* their knowledge to, for example, their weekly budget.

The theory of central coherence
Central coherence is the tendency to process information holistically: to be able to integrate details and see the 'big picture'. You may have seen the activity below on the Internet (the answer is at the end of the paragraph):

Activity 3
Q. How many letters 'f' can you see in this sentence?

Finished files are the results of years of scientific study combined with the experience of years.

I must emphasize that this exercise is in no way diagnostic! But it is interesting to see how our minds tackle tasks of this sort. Most of you will have found your-selves being drawn into the *meaning* of the sentence (and therefore ignored the word 'of'); our minds are predisposed to search for meaning. Some of you looked at the details and did exactly what was required: counted the 'f's'. (The answer is that there are six. Look again if you need to, particularly at the minor words!)

This activity highlights a thinking style, but researchers have found that people with ASD often focus on the details at the expense of the 'big picture'; that is, they tend to have weak central coherence. This can cause problems if you need to be able to combine information from, for example, a social situation in order to decide what your response should be. If you've been struck by the fact that three people in the room have the same shade of red jumper, then you may miss the prevailing emotion (e.g. excitement, grief) and so appear to be uninterested or even uncaring.

The biological theories

Firstly, it is important to dispense with what ASD is not: there is no evidence to support the notion that it is caused by bad parenting or by mothers who are reportedly 'emotionally remote'. While behavioural or emotional difficulties have a different origin and can, to some extent, mirror some of the features of autism (e.g. social withdrawal), it has been established that ASD itself is an organic condition. This section looks very briefly at some of the organic aspects of ASD.

The genetic perspective
While it is unlikely that researchers will discover a 'gene' for autism, there is considerable evidence that ASD does have a genetic basis, probably involving a number of interacting genes. Where a child in a particular family has ASD, the increased likelihood of siblings being similarly affected is approximately 50 times higher (Jordan, 1999) than for children in unaffected families. Conversely, being the identical twin of someone with ASD does not guarantee that you will also be affected – demonstrating the complexity of gene expression and inherited potential.

It would appear, however, that individuals may be born with a genetic predisposition to develop ASD, and that other factors, present before birth or in infancy, may exist or interact both with the genes and with each other to bring this about. These mechanisms are not fully understood and exhaustive research is continuing to establish the links between the different elements discussed. Some of the possibilities being explored are listed below:

♦ pre-, neo- and post-natal difficulties;

♦ chemical imbalances in the brain;

♦ metabolic abnormalities (e.g. to do with the digestion of certain foods) affecting the chemical balance in the brain and body, particularly the bowel;

♦ abnormalities (i.e. neurological) in brain structure;

♦ abnormalities in brain function.

Given this variability, it is difficult to cite a particular cause, or to analyse how the different dimensions might combine and express themselves in any one individual. The eventual picture is certain to be a complex one.

The link with other conditions
ASD is sometimes present as part of a wider diagnosis, and – as highlighted above – this is often where a genetic, metabolic, neurological or language and communication condition has been identified. Again, this is highly variable, and all the following conditions can exist with or without ASD:

♦ Fragile X syndrome;

♦ phenylketonuria;

♦ tuberous sclerosis;

♦ Rett's syndrome;

♦ Landau-Kleffner syndrome;

♦ disintegrative disorder (usually metabolic);

♦ epilepsy;

♦ general learning difficulties.

There is also a considerable degree of overlap with other specific diagnoses that affect children's learning abilities, for example:

♦ attention deficit hyperactive disorder and attention deficit disorder (ADHD/ADD);

♦ dyspraxia;

♦ dyslexia;

♦ disorders of attention, motor coordination and perception (DAMP).

Some conditions appear to mirror the main characteristics of ASD closely and expert analysis is needed
to tease out just what the nature of the child's difficulties are. For example:

♦ receptive language disorder (sometimes known as
specific language impairment, particularly where
there is no accompanying learning difficulty);

♦ attachment disorder;

♦ emotional and behavioural difficulties (EBD);

♦ selective mutism.

Lastly, some confusion continues to arise from the
lack of consistency in the way ASD may be labelled or
described. There has been a tendency (particularly in
the past when the use of the word 'autism' was
avoided) to refer to 'social communication disorder'. A
complex debate has for some time surrounded the use
of the term **semantic-pragmatic language disorder**
(now usually referred to as **pragmatic language
impairment**) and whether it constitutes a separate
condition, or whether it provides an alternative description. Speech and language therapists may use this
term.

Other terms, such as **pathological demand avoid-
ance syndrome** and **non-verbal learning disability**
may be used to describe conditions with particular
characteristics that are felt to differentiate them from
classic autism or Asperger's syndrome. Again, there is

debate as to whether they should be viewed separately or included within the autistic spectrum. Just as problematic are the individuals who have been described as having 'autistic tendencies or traits': an individual *has,* or *does not have* autism according to the Triad of Impairments. However, we can probably all think of people who behave similarly but who may not meet the criteria. The term **pervasive developmental disorder – not otherwise specified** (PDD-NOS) is sometimes used for these individuals.

It is clear that there is a lack of clarity regarding both the causes and the appropriate ways to describe ASD. There is not room here to discuss these issues in more depth, but the interested reader will find further general information in Chapter 7.

Individual variation: the same but different

The common factor for all people diagnosed with an autistic spectrum disorder is the Triad of Impairments outlined at the beginning of the chapter. It has also been noted, however, that individuals differ greatly from each other. This section aims to describe some of the main dimensions for variation.

Severity

The autistic spectrum encompasses people who are profoundly affected by their autism to people with Asperger's syndrome who appear little more than mildly eccentric. The more severely they experience the impairments of the Triad, the less they are likely to seek relationships with others, the more problematic their language and communication skills are (to the extent that they may not develop spoken language skills), the more they are rigidly resistant to change and experience significant sensory differences. Conversely, Asperger's syndrome, in which people tend to experience less marked difficulties in these areas (but may be more likely to have motor clumsiness) may mistakenly be seen as having 'a mild form of autism'. However, feeling socially isolated and generally misunderstood is likely to cause individuals significant level of stress and anxiety, and should therefore not be viewed – and is certainly not experienced – as mild in any sense.

Cognitive abilities

While it is believed that cognitive impairment (i.e. learning difficulty) is strongly associated with autism (affecting over half the people with ASD) there are many problems identifying both the presence and degree of such difficulty. There are several reasons for this.

1. It can be difficult to establish the extent to which an individual's ASD interferes with their ability to learn. For example, their social understanding (e.g. their understanding of other people's minds) may prevent them from following a story in literacy hour.

2. The norms provided on current standardized assessments (cognitive and language tests) are developed from testing the 'normal' population and do not take the learning and response styles of people with autism into account.

3. The cognitive skills profiles of people with ASD are likely to be uneven (this may also be referred to as 'spiky'): that is, they may be very good at some things (e.g. mathematics, science) but find others very difficult (e.g. history, which involves both literacy and time concepts).

4. Many more people with Asperger's syndrome (and PDD-NOS), without additional learning difficulties, are now being identified. This suggests that the high percentages cited for learning difficulties accompanying ASD may be more applicable to the more classic forms of autism.

Personality

Individuals with ASD are just that: individuals! In the same way that any person brings their own strengths – and struggles – to a given situation, so too people with ASD bring their own combination of factors. Added to which, the way that families cope with the diagnosis and support their family member is also highly variable, and can contribute to different outcomes in their successful integration into society.

The next chapter focuses on the assessment and diagnosis of ASD. Chapters 3 to 6 address the practical strategies that relate to an understanding of ASD and – in particular – to an understanding of the individual pupil. I have provided general information, and although different key stages and special educational settings may be cited, most strategies can be adapted for the pupils' ages and stages of development as appropriate. Chapter 7 contains further information and resources, and any references to books throughout can be found there.

First, a quiz!

ASD: a short quiz

Answer true or false to the following statements. (The answers are below, but can also be found throughout the text.)

1. Autism may be accompanied by epilepsy.   T / F
2. There are more females than males with autism.   T / F
3. Over half of all people with autism also have a learning difficulty.   T / F
4. Autism can occur randomly throughout the population.   T / F
5. Autism does not have an organic or biological basis.   T / F
6. People with autism tend to have similar personalities.   T / F
7. People with autism find it difficult to imagine other people's thoughts.   T / F
8. People with autism find it easy to carry out several tasks at once.   T / F
9. Autism can be caused by poor parenting.   T / F
10. Autism can co-occur with other conditions.   T / F

Answers:
1-T; 2-F; 3-T; 4-T; 5-F; 6-F; 7-T; 8-F; 9-F; 10-T

2

Assessment and Diagnosis

Throughout this chapter it will be assumed that the person being assessed, with a view to clarifying the diagnosis, is a child. Parents, rather than the individual with ASD, will therefore be placed in the central role of contributing to that process. The male pronoun will be used in referring to the child throughout this book, reflecting the higher incidence of ASD in boys and men.

The multi-disciplinary approach

It is now generally accepted among professionals that no one person on their own should or can give a diagnosis of ASD. While appreciating the very high levels of anxiety experienced by parents during the assessment process, as well as their pressing need for someone to tell them what the problem is, it is essential that the professionals involved act as a team – even if this means the process does take longer. The reasons for this should be obvious:

♦ Several professional perspectives (e.g. cognitive and learning abilities; language and communication skills; motor and sensory skills; and medical and developmental histories) are necessary in order to reach a diagnosis. A diagnosis cannot be formulated on a single perspective or set of opinions.

♦ The child's abilities and needs must be assessed over time, and within a range of settings, for example, a classroom, home, group situations and on an individual basis.

♦ It would be, and is, extremely distressing for parents if one professional gives his or her opinion, only for a conflicting opinion to be given by the next person who sees the child.

Activity 1
Below is a list of most of the professionals who are likely to be involved in the process of assessment and diagnosis. Before you look at it, try making your own list and see how well it compares.

Who should be involved?

The number of professionals who may see any individual child during assessment will vary, but may include:

♦ paediatrician (acute and/or community);

♦ child and adolescent psychiatrist;

♦ educational psychologist;

♦ clinical psychologist;

♦ speech and language therapist;

♦ specialist teaching service.

Although less likely to contribute directly to the diagnosis, other involved professionals may include:

♦ class teacher and teaching assistant;

♦ social worker;

♦ occupational therapist;

♦ physiotherapist;

♦ members of the primary health care team (e.g. GP, health visitor).

All professionals involved in the diagnosis should, ideally, have some specialist knowledge of ASD.

A final diagnosis depends upon the extent to which the child's difficulties meet the criteria outlined in the Triad of Impairments. The criteria are detailed in both the international diagnostic manuals: the *International Classification of Diseases* (ICD-10) and the *Diagnostic and Statistical Manual of Mental Disorders* (DSM-IV) (see Chapter 7, p. 96).

Methods of assessment

No single test or assessment can lead to a diagnosis of ASD, but there are several methods and many assessments available that help to tease out the nature of the difficulties experienced by an individual child. The main types of assessment are described below. For details of the assessment methods named, refer to the lists of resources in Chapter 7.

Direct assessment

This involves a period of time spent with the child, asking them to carry out a series of tasks, and observing how they go about completing those tasks. Whether or not the tester even gains the child's attention and cooperation is, of itself, an important dimension. People who regularly work with children with ASD are aware that (a) the presence of a 'barrier' in the communication between the tester and the child, and (b) the child's ability to follow instructions or respond to questions, need to be taken into consideration. Direct assessments are usually complex and lengthy to administer, and specialist training in their use is sometimes required.

Examples of this type of assessment include:

♦ the Psycho-Educational Profile – Revised (PEP–R);

♦ the Autism Diagnostic Observation Schedule (ADOS). (A pre-school version of this also exists: the Pre-Linguistic Autism Diagnostic Observation Schedule (PL-ADOS).)

Diagnostic interviews

These are usually carried out by specifically trained professionals, and conducted with – preferably – both parents, or a parent and one other person who knows the child well. This ensures a higher level of recall from past events, as well as greater accuracy about the more subtle aspects. Useful as these interviews are for obtaining a complete history of the child's development, they should never be used in isolation:

observation and assessment of the child is both essential and crucial.

Examples of such interviews include:

♦ the Autism Diagnostic Interview (ADI): often used alongside the ADOS;

♦ the Diagnostic Interview for Social and Communication Disorders (DISCO).

Checklists and profiles

These allow for observation in many different settings, by different people, and usually cover the essential aspects of the Triad of Impairments. They tend to be lengthy and time-consuming, however, and do not always help to distinguish between, for example, ASD and language impairment or emotional and behavioural disorders.

There is a wide range of such checklists, and only a sample is listed here:

♦ the Childhood Autism Rating Scale (CARS);

♦ the Gilliam Rating Scale (GARS);

♦ the Children's Communication Checklist (CCC-2);

♦ the *Autistic Continuum: An Assessment and Intervention Schedule* (Aarons and Gittens, 1992).

Above all, experienced professionals will develop, over time, the ability to 'intuit' the strengths and needs of each individual child as they carry out the assessment procedures available to them. Intuition is, of course, never sufficient on its own – but most would acknowledge that such experience acts as a guide throughout the process of reaching consensus between themselves and the child's parents.

Activity

Using the knowledge gained from this and the previous chapter, have a go at jotting down a list of the difficulties you might expect a child with ASD to present with. Use the difficulties outlined in the Triad of Impairments to structure your checklist. You may be able to do this by thinking about a child that you know.

You might find it useful to do this as a group activity.

When you've finished, look at the checklists provided on one of the next two pages (mainstream and special provision) and see how yours compares!

See if you can complete the appropriate checklists for the children in the case studies in Chapter 1.

Autistic Spectrum Disorders

Mini-checklist (1) – Special Schools

This list is intended to be only a rapid 'screen' for pupils in schools for children with severe learning difficulties, and to establish whether further investigations to assess the presence of an autistic spectrum disorder (i.e. classic, or 'Kanner's', type) are required.

Appears aloof and lacks interest in their surroundings	
Does not interact with others	
Does not attempt to communicate	
Does not respond to his/her name	
Does not respond to verbal comments, including greetings	
Avoids eye contact	
Resists sitting down for circle time or snack time	
May place hands over ears	
May rock back and forth and/or flap hands vigorously	
May scream without *apparent* cause	
Does not demonstrate pretend play or other imaginative skills	
May stare at lights or other visual stimuli	
May demonstrate unusual and obsessive behaviours	
May be insensitive to pain	
May be hypersensitive to sounds, tastes and textures	
May become highly distressed at unexpected changes to routine	
May resist trying new experiences	
May demonstrate a special (or 'splinter') skill, e.g. reading ability	

Mini-checklist (2) – Mainstream Schools

The following are possible indicators that a mainstream school child may have an autistic spectrum disorder (including Asperger's syndrome).

This checklist does not indicate a diagnosis.

May appear aloof and lack interest in their surroundings, *or*	
May interact with others, but has difficulty doing so appropriately	
May make limited attempts to communicate, e.g. to ask for help	
May resist sitting down in group situations	
May not respond to group instructions, but may respond to his/her name	
May not respond to social comments, e.g. greetings	
May have difficulty knowing how to talk appropriately to adults	
May display outbursts without *apparent* cause	
May find eye contact difficult	
May appear to be not listening or attending	
May experience difficulties understanding and using language	
May take longer to respond to comments or questions	
May have limited understanding of social skills, e.g. waiting, turn-taking	
May not be able to appreciate jokes or sarcasm	
May have limited understanding of body language and facial expressions	
May have limited pretend play or other imaginative skills	

Autistic Spectrum Disorders

May demonstrate unusual, repetitive or obsessive behaviours	
May have special and repetitive interests	
May have difficulty with unexpected changes to routine	
May have difficulty knowing how to begin or end a task	
May resist trying new experiences	
May know letters/numbers out of proportion to other skills	
May have difficulty organizing themselves, e.g. with equipment	
May have poor gross and/or fine motor skills	
May make 'odd' body movements, e.g. hand flapping or wringing	
May make sudden sounds/noises	
May experience touch or pain in unusual ways	
May be hypersensitive to (loud) sounds, tastes, textures, smells	

In addition to the items above, in older pupils these difficulties may appear in more subtle forms.

May find it difficult to see another person's point of view	
May see things in very 'black and white' terms	
May appear to lack 'common sense'	
May find the unstructured parts of the school day difficult, e.g. lunchtimes	
May have difficulties with inference and abstract ideas	
May have difficulties generalizing skills from one context to another	
May behave differently at home as compared with behaviour in school	

Why label?

Richard Exley, who has Asperger's syndrome, believes that diagnosis should be seen to act as a form of 'signpost not a label'. There is much debate about whether it is helpful to the child, and to the parents, to give a 'label' – that is, a firm diagnosis including all the implications that accompany it. Some parents feel that a label is a vital step toward obtaining the resources and support their child needs. Others feel that such a label might stigmatize their child and lead to inappropriate judgements and predictions about his/her abilities and future potential.

A label need not be a fixed, static entity. Rather, it should provide parents and professionals alike with the dynamic knowledge and understanding that such a 'label' implies: in other words, what direction do we now take in order to meet this child's *needs*?

Many adults who have been belatedly diagnosed with ASD, as our understanding about its more subtle forms (e.g. Asperger's syndrome) has developed, have expressed a profound relief that their struggles have been identified and that their feelings of alienation do indeed have a reason. Sadly, for them, while the eventual diagnosis does explain their difficulties, their school lives are behind them and the help that they needed so badly was not forthcoming. This is expressed particularly poignantly in Clare Sainsbury's book, *Martian in the Playground* (2000).

For adults diagnosed in later life, these revelations sometimes arise as the difficulties their own children, or grandchildren, have are identified – with all the accompanying pain of guilt about future generations as well as their own lost opportunities that this brings. Luke Jackson (2002), author at age 13 of a book for his peers, strongly champions the rights of people with ASD to be told of their diagnosis as early as possible. This must be done through close, careful and positive consultation with the parents, and with a great deal of support to explore what the diagnosis means (see Chapter 7 for details of a helpful book, *I Am Special*, by Peter Vermeulen). In addition, there needs to be encouragement for the child to see diagnosis neither as a convenient peg upon which to hang every aspect of their lives, nor as a way of excusing themselves of personal responsibility.

Luke's book, besides being useful to his peers, is of great benefit to professionals who have an enormous amount to learn from people with ASD. Several people now provide support or give talks (e.g. Richard Exley or Ros Blackburn), or have written books (e.g. Donna Williams and Temple Grandin), describing their experiences and perceptions. There is a list of such resources in Chapter 7.

Teachers' assessments and pupils' learning styles

Assessment and diagnosis provides the signpost, or direction, proposed by Richard Exley, and is therefore useful as a basis for planning teaching and individual targets. Key strategies for supporting children with ASD will be discussed in the next four chapters.

Unlike the debate surrounding the use of assessment procedures leading to a diagnosis, the requirement to assess and establish the learning styles and needs of pupils with ASD is more apparent. Without an understanding of a pupil's learning style and individual strengths, their access to the curriculum is likely to be impeded. Children with ASD do have highly specific needs that necessitate consistency and organization in the way they are met, to enable them to access the curriculum and make maximum progress (educationally and socially). The advice and strategies outlined in Chapters 3, 4, 5 and 6 will focus, not merely on the difficulties that accompany the condition, but also on its inherent strengths.

More broadly – and, hopefully, of encouragement to teachers – the key strategies largely amount to the implementation of good classroom practice. The strategies that work for children with ASD often also work for children with a range of other difficulties such as language impairment, emotional and behavioural difficulties and ADHD, for example; although some of the behaviourist-based strategies that might work for the last two groups do not always work for children with ASD. It is possible, therefore, to make adjustments to the classroom and to the teaching methods adopted to develop the learning abilities of children with ASD while continuing to cater for the other children in the same class.

What do we tell the other children?

This is obviously a highly sensitive area. Whether, and how, you tell other children about the difficulties the child with ASD is experiencing depends on several factors:

♦ the age of the child when diagnosed;

♦ the nature of the diagnosis and the confidence with which it has been given;

♦ whether the child is old enough, or aware enough, to have been told of their own diagnosis (again, refer to Luke Jackson's views);

♦ the need for other people to know the diagnosis, and if so, who should be told;

♦ how much (and how little) it is necessary to tell others.

As a general rule, it seems to be best to tell other children just as much as they need to know and no more. And to do this it is **essential** to have the permission of either the parents or – preferably – the parents and the child. I have done this successfully in various ways, and here are two examples.

1. Tell a selected group of peers (usually older peers, i.e. late Key Stage 2, Key Stages 3 and 4) so that they can look out for and support the pupil as a group. This level of support is too much responsibility for just one pupil, who would be likely to have considerable anxieties about his own peer group status. The pupil with ASD may or may not wish to be present during the discussions.

2. In the absence of the pupil with ASD (but with his permission), tell the whole class or form group. This allows for a question and answer session that can be invaluable in eliminating some surprisingly odd ideas! It also gives an opportunity for specific messages to be given regarding the pupil's own needs;

for example, 'Please leave me alone if I'm walking along the lines in the playground'.

The word 'autism' does not have to be used; substituting a variety of phrases (e.g. 'trouble talking to other people') will do just as well, particularly for younger children. The child might prefer that no one comes and asks about it afterwards, he usually just wants other children to accept the situation without further inquisition. The child who does want to talk incessantly about his diagnosis (and even use it as an excuse for bad behaviour) may need, gently, to be discouraged.

Making this decision is a delicate process and requires great sensitivity. Do discuss it with the child's parents and the supporting professionals before any action is taken.

3

Teaching Approaches: Classroom Organization

This chapter aims to enable class and head teachers to make the best use of two of their main teaching resources – people and space. Teamwork, once established, provides the vital consistency needed by all the children in the classroom and particularly by the child with ASD. Similarly, the layout of the room and its equipment are important factors in providing 'safety and sameness' in the environment for pupils with ASD. While these strategies will need regular review and occasional adaptation, once they are implemented successfully they should support the main tasks of teaching – access to the curriculum and academic progress – without having to be regularly 'reinvented'.

It is also extremely important that all school and classroom staff, and – where possible – midday assistants, take opportunities to access joint training in the nature of ASD and on the strategies required to support children with ASD. Sharing training and knowledge with the speech and language therapist (SLT) is also strongly advised.

Teaching and learning support assistants

It is acknowledged that there are potentially controversial management issues to do with the deployment of teaching assistants (TAs) and learning support assistants (LSAs); however, it is not within the scope of this book to address them here. Not all classes have a TA assigned to them, and typically, mainstream classes from Key Stage 2 upwards will, at best, share TA time with another class. Most classes in special schools will have access to at least one TA. By no means all children with ASD have access to a designated LSA.

Since most people occupying the position of TA or LSA are usually women, the female pronoun will be used throughout this book, with apologies to those men who are TAs and LSAs.

The role of teaching assistants and learning support assistants

The main role of TAs and LSAs is to support the class teacher and enable him or her to meet the needs of *all* the pupils in the class. This statement may seem more obvious where the class has access to a TA, and where the class teacher will probably plan carefully and jointly, when possible, in order to make the best use of her time and skills. This is likely to involve, for example, small group and individual work with pupils.

The presence in a class of a pupil with ASD can mean that the TA's time is spent supporting him as well as other pupils. This can sometimes put quite a strain on the class resources and may well be a factor in the discussions held about the need for some support hours to be allocated to the pupil, and an LSA subsequently being appointed. However, contradictory as it may seem when an individual pupil is involved, the role of the LSA remains the same as was previously stated: to support the class teacher and enable him or her to meet the needs of *all* the pupils in the class.

This needs looking at in a bit more detail. The initial reason for an LSA to be appointed is because of the needs of an individual pupil; this is for a number of reasons, all or some of which may be present:

♦ the pupil is struggling to access the curriculum;

♦ the pupil is underachieving, that is, failing to make progress in line with his *own* potential (and not necessarily that of the class as a whole);

♦ the needs of the pupil involve and monopolize an excessive amount of the class teacher's or TA's time in order to achieve his own potential;

♦ the pupil represents a risk to his own safety, or that of the other pupils in the class, due to his difficulties controlling his behaviour.

The latter reason, particularly, may also prompt the allocation of some support hours for the out of class times, the 'jungle' times that playtimes and lunchtimes can certainly be. This time can be allocated to a suitably trained midday assistant.

Activity 1

Before looking at the list below, think about what an LSA might do to provide practical support for the child with ASD, and see if you can write down some of the key issues. Again, this might be better done as a group activity, and may be particularly valuable as a shared activity for the class teacher and the LSA.

Given the comments above regarding the shared use of the LSA's time, she should, with experience, be able to develop the skills to judge when it is time to step in and provide direct one-to-one support for the pupil with ASD. Here are some of the key issues and areas for support. The list is not definitive, and there are many possibilities. The language and communication aspects of the points below are covered in Chapter 5.

♦ Help the pupil to develop effective listening and attention skills and habits, particularly in group situations.

♦ Provide the pupil with additional opportunities to process and follow the instructions the teacher has given the whole class group.

♦ Enable the pupil to formulate his responses and to say them at the appropriate time.

♦ Plan and organize the task he has been given (more details about this in Chapter 4, p. 60).

♦ Carry out and complete the task he has been given (again, more in Chapter 4, p. 63).

♦ To support the pupil in developing his independent learning skills (see below).

♦ Enable to pupil to develop his play skills, social communication skills (particularly at 'jungle' times) and peer group friendships to the best of his potential.

Encouraging independence

However, as noted in the list above, the experienced and skilful LSA will also acquire an understanding of when to step *back* and allow the pupil to develop his own, independent learning skills. This will only develop over time, but one of the primary functions of an LSA is exactly that: to engender maximum independent learning and social skills.

But, LSAs will then achieve their own redundancy, you cry! Yes, to some extent that is the case, but it is equally important to note that, in practice, independence is usually only partially acquired, or, if acquired at primary school may evaporate on the transfer to secondary. Nevertheless, that is the ultimate goal; and an LSA who attempts to remain with the child at all times is misinterpreting her role. Supporting the teacher by, for example, working with the child with ASD in a small group, or working with another group of children entirely, is an excellent use of the LSA's time.

At regular intervals, and often at the annual review of the pupil's statement of special educational needs, it may be necessary to re-examine the allocation of the support hours provided by the LSA. It is crucial that the way these hours are used is analysed carefully, with a detailed and specific outline of the purpose of any additional hours that might be allocated. Given the above comments, about engendering the pupil's independent learning skills, the idea that 'more is always better' may not apply.

The inclusive classroom – the layout

A place for everything

Some years ago, supermarkets and clothing chain stores hit upon the idea of moving all the goods in their shops around at intervals in order to – we're told – maintain the excitement and motivation supposedly inherent in the shopping experience! Presumably someone stays up all night to do this, as the shopper usually arrives at opening time to find a completely new layout. They may feel immensely excited and motivated; or, as in my case, flee in panic to find an alternative supermarket that does keep everything in the same place.

A lot of us feel this way (and we like to pack our own shopping too). It does not mean that we are on the autistic spectrum (remember, diagnosis implies difficulties in all three dimensions of the Triad of Impairments); there is nothing that people with ASD do that the rest of us don't do at some time – it is the extent and duration that is important. But many people in the general population do share similar feelings and anxieties about change, and we all adapt to change at different speeds and in different ways. Now, by thinking of any changes that disturb you, and imagining those feelings of anxiety and confusion magnified many, many times, you may have some idea of what unexpected change might feel like for people with ASD. People with ASD are sometimes distressed by the unexpected and unpredictable, and sameness is usually highly comforting. This varies from one individual to another: from Hannah's intense dislike of changes

41

to her mother's hairstyle to Daniel's need to talk and talk about the same topic.

In practice, and in terms of planning classroom space, the obvious solution is to ensure the minimum of change possible (see also Chapter 6 on managing change). As you will see with other key strategies, this does not amount to making an unnecessary concession, any more than, for example, providing a ramp for a wheelchair user is an unnecessary concession. You will need to evaluate and choose from the following strategies those that are relevant for your own setting (i.e. primary, secondary or special school).

1. Draw a seating plan for the class and make sure they do sit in the same places. At primary school, this can mean different (but consistent) places for different lessons (e.g. literacy hour) and at secondary school the pupils can be seated as the teacher requires for each subject.

2. Designate areas of the classroom/school for specific purposes, for example a quiet corner or place to go at times of anxiety and overload; the same place, or arrangement, each day for eating snack or lunch. It may be possible to be particularly creative with space use in special schools and small classes.

3. In primary schools, make use of the furniture to show the pupils what the next activity is. For example, you can put the chairs in a semicircle for register and news-time, and then turn them round, in a straight line and facing the other way, for literacy hour. In special schools, the consistent use of the same tablecloth for snack time, for example,

means that you can use the same table the pupils were doing artwork on a moment ago.

4. Keep all the classroom equipment (e.g. pencils, scrap paper, rulers, etc.) tidy, in the same place and stored in separate containers.

A place for the child

It is sometimes useful for the pupil with ASD to have his own seat away from the other children. This should not be viewed negatively (or even deliberately adopted!) as 'exclusion within an inclusive environment' – children with ASD find it very difficult to share their space with others all day and can derive great relief from being able to sit apart. Given individual variation, this might not be necessary, and only a thorough knowledge of the child will help you make that decision.

It may be worth considering, particularly when the pupil first joins the class, whether the use of screens at the side of his table or desk would help him. It may mean that he can concentrate better on his own work, as he has not got to worry about seeing the other pupils, or being seen by them. The screens and the wall he is facing should be as plain and free from distraction as possible, which is a difficult concept for teachers to implement, as we would normally be doing everything we could to stimulate a child and make his surroundings fun and inviting. 'Fun' and 'inviting' may, however, be quite threatening to children with ASD and can even result in distressing levels of sensory overload for them.

Introducing the pupil with ASD to the idea of sitting and working alongside others should be phased into his day gradually. This development can be viewed as a target in itself and included in his individual education plan (IEP) when it becomes appropriate. To begin with, the screens could be moved, one at a time, until he is used to working without them. The next move is to bring one child, who should be mature, quiet and socially competent, over to the pupil's table to work with him there. Do not force any interaction at this stage. Bit by bit, a little group (of similar children) can eventually grow, so that he becomes used to pupils chatting and working round him. Only then can he be moved to sit with the main class group, and for periods that increase in length gradually. It is essential that during this process the child is only required to carry out tasks that are easy, motivating and achievable, and only for short periods. He can only learn one skill at a time!

For more detail on practical strategies and adaptations of classroom space refer to a book by Theo Peeters (1997), details of which are in Chapter 7.

Activity 2

Think about your own classroom, or the class you take where there is a pupil with ASD, and draw a basic plan of it. Think about the present layout and where everything is kept.

Where does the pupil sit at the moment? What are his needs in terms of classroom and personal space? What changes and improvements could you make, in the light of the information above?

N.B. You will need to think about *how* to introduce these changes! (See Chapter 6)

Even if the child with ASD does not need a separate place to work, sitting with the rest of the class group can sometimes be quite a problem. Feeling overloaded from being in the midst of the group (at carpet-time, for example) they may produce the space they need by using physical means, such as kicking, pushing, and so on. Or, since they often have little idea of the space required by others, they may lean on or over the other children, stroke their hair or touch their faces. If they need to get up and walk away from the group (e.g. to point to something on the board) they may trample across the other children, stepping on legs and hands, quite oblivious to the effect they are having. Needless to say, this is not deliberate unkindness – they lack the empathy skills to realize that this is unpleasant for others (see Chapter 5).

If the child has been seated at the edge of the group, even right next to the teacher, the problems may still persist, or different problems may arise. Once at the edge of the group, the child may take the opportunity to turn his back on everyone else and will not be able to listen or attend. When I first visit a class I often request that the child I have come to see is not pointed out to me. I can usually spot him: he's the one facing away from the group, fiddling with something on a nearby shelf, or his own laces, humming to himself. Whatever the teacher is saying is of no more (and possibly even of less) interest to him than the noise of, say, the computer humming.

Other difficulties are more to do with communication (again, see Chapter 5), and may include speaking out to the teacher in an inappropriately familiar way; difficulty taking his turn (either by refusing or interrupting); and general disruption in the form of, for example, noises and language unrelated to the activity.

The strategies that almost always work are surprisingly straightforward. Below are some examples.

♦ At carpet-time, consider providing the child with a carpet square (obtainable from most carpet stores as samples). If he has a clear, visual, designated space to sit, he will often simply stay there. If the difficulties persist, then using a 'special' chair may serve the same purpose. Teachers often feel that this is singling the child out, so designating a regular seating space for all the children (particularly at secondary school) can get round this.

♦ Involve your class in choosing a 'special' object, such as a beany toy, or a large fir-cone. Introduce the idea that the children can only talk when they are holding the object and not at any other time. This can be particularly practical at circle time. Teachers have often observed to us, after trying this, that *all* the children benefit from learning the rules of good turn-taking.

♦ With his parents' permission, take a photograph of the child in a sitting, listening pose. Place the photograph on the whiteboard (or somewhere nearby) where he can see it. If he fidgets, point to the photo and briefly remind him why it's there: 'Good sitting, Daniel'. If this is not sufficient, introduce a reward system so that if he sits well (for short periods to start with – encourage the habit of success!) he gets, for example, a tick, or a smiley face. A certain number of ticks/faces will result in a small reward, agreed either in the classroom (e.g. five more minutes on the computer) or at home (discuss this with his parents). (See the end of Chapter 4.) Again, teachers often find that this helps some of their other less attentive children.

♦ At Key Stages 3 and 4 a more age appropriate reward system might be introduced, and monitored by the Special Educational Needs Coordinator (SENCO), head of year or form tutor. Reports from all the pupil's teachers can contribute to their evaluations of his behaviour and coping skills.

♦ Estimate out how long a younger pupil is able to sit before he begins to fidget. It might be that he can manage for the first five minutes, in which case remove him from the group after four minutes to a designated place to work quietly. He should know that this is not a punishment, merely his place to sit after this length of time. Gradually increase the time that he can remain in the group. The important point here is that he is being removed from the group on your terms and not on his – that is, not because he has had an outburst. He is likely to find being removed for an outburst highly rewarding and well worth doing again!

♦ Older pupils may benefit from being provided with an agreed signal showing that they need a break (e.g. a red card). This can look like an 'invitation to skive' – but in my experience it is seldom abused. Sometimes having a small object (e.g. a little ball of Blu-tak, or a flap of paper) to fiddle with can – far from distracting the pupil – help to maintain his attention and help him to feel calm.

Playtimes and lunch breaks

These 'jungle times' are often the most difficult for both the child and for the staff to manage! The potential for confusion to occur, and for everyone else to mis-interpret the sources of confusion, is significant. It is probably also the time when there is least supervision available to help the child and monitor what he's doing. The pupil with ASD may actually find playtimes, the very times that other children relish and look forward to, the most difficult part of his school day.

The child may develop his own strategies for coping with this stressful time. For example, he may choose an area of the playground and walk repetitively up and down one of the lines. There is an awful lot of space out there, and by confining himself to one bit of the playground he can reduce those feelings of being over-whelmed. This strategy, as long as the child himself is happy with it, is probably quite a good one; as you will see later (Chapter 4), it is important to let him be 'autis-tic' sometimes. It may be helpful to find a way of letting the other children know why the pupil with ASD needs to do this and not have to talk to anyone (refer back to Chapter 2, and the section on telling other people about the needs of the child with ASD, p. 33–5).

On the other hand, the child may view the space as highly stimulating and become over-excited, running around aimlessly and banging into people. Behaviour that can seem to be physically aggressive may have a variety of hidden purposes, however. In one school, when a boy with ASD was asked why he had walked up to and hit another child, he replied, 'Because I wanted him to chase me'.

A brief glance across the playground may suggest that a child is playing well with his peers and having lots of healthy fun. One 7-year-old boy was seen, initially, to be having a great time 'joining in' with a group of boys playing football. A longer period of observation revealed that he was simply dashing about, never even close to the ball, and then diving into a roll on the ground – just as he had seen professional soccer players doing on the television! However, when his imitation of these routines also began to include barging into the other children and even kicking them, they complained about him to the person on duty and attempted to exclude him from their game.

The following brief pen-portrait might help to illustrate further the kind of difficulties children encounter, along with some of the solutions.

Callum entered Year 1 at a mainstream primary school having been excluded from a private nursery for 'aggressive behaviour'. Outside in the playground Callum's difficulties became apparent. His own creative imagination was limited, but he spent a lot of time looking at videos and books, and enjoyed acting the stories out many times over. Copying one of his favourites, he would become a bear at playtime and then chase other children around the playground, growling, scratching and biting them. At this stage neither the children, nor the staff, realized that he was being a bear and all they perceived was the apparent aggression.

Some discussion with Callum and his mother revealed that he was acting out a story; but clearly, whatever the reasons for his behaviour, he could not be allowed to continue hurting the other children. A story was found for him that depicted a child playing hopscotch. His mother agreed to show Callum how to play hopscotch at home and she then came into school so that he could learn how to play hopscotch in the school playground (see Chapter 6 and the transference of skills from one context to another). He was allocated a small, quiet area of the playground in which to play his game and shown the limits of this area. Inevitably, other children soon came to see what he was playing and they were helped and encouraged to join in, but only one at a time. (This also had the hidden advantage of fostering their eagerness to have their turn.) Callum was able to tolerate and enjoy this structured and limited interaction with one child at a time. Once this was established, whoever was on playground duty was able to keep an eye on the game and monitor the involvement of the other children, alongside carrying out their duties watching the other children.

If things in the playground do get too much for him, then a place (a 'safe haven') in the school building where the child can play quietly (e.g. with lego, the train track) might be better. This could be implemented on the same principle as the planned removal from the class group at carpet-time: set an initial (and achievable) time limit, and gradually increase the time spent in the playground before moving on to the safe haven. Again, unless the child with ASD does just need the time alone, one other child could be carefully introduced into the safe haven. Make sure that the other child is happy with this, and that both sets of parents know about the arrangement. It could be done on a rota basis, with a (limited) series of children. Clearly, there are also implications for the staffing of this arrangement.

One last word on this topic: meal time itself is also a potential area of difficulty. Many of the ideas raised here regarding the designated use of space also apply to meal times and, a regular routine should be set up for the child. Letting him have a regular place at the front of the queue may also be helpful. If the dinner hall is too noisy, so that the child is overwhelmed and unable to eat, he could be seated in a separate, quiet area; although, again, this is obviously dependent on the provision of staffing and supervision.

Reducing sensory overload in the environment

One of the main difficulties in accommodating the needs of the child with ASD in this respect is simultaneously managing to accommodate the needs of the other children in the class. The aim is always to achieve a balance where possible, and to be aware of the need to make appropriate modifications. Here, again, the strategy of the 'safe haven' can be introduced alongside your management of the immediate environment, so that the child has somewhere to go in order to reduce the overload he is experiencing at any particular time.

It is useful to think of these difficulties by looking at each of the senses in turn. This is an area where it can be necessary to be quite creative in devising strategies to cope with these problems. Some examples are given below, but remember, there will be considerable individual variation.

Sight
This aspect has already been raised in relation to the use of screens in a separate working area to hide both other children and busy classroom displays. Bright

colours and patterns are likely to be distracting – I have worn pattern-free (specifically stripe-free) clothes since working with a boy who was unable to do anything other than gaze intently at the stripes. Be aware of the effects of lighting, as strip lighting can be particularly trying. People with ASD are usually strongly visual in their processing style (see Chapter 4) and visual images will hold their attention far more than what they can hear.

Sound
Again, there is a good deal of variation here. Some children do not even flinch when very loud noises are made right next to them, but may become distressed by an apparently minor sound, such as Velcro being separated. Children with ASD (particularly Kanner's type) can often be seen with their fingers or thumbs in their ears, body rocking with distress from the level of environmental noise. A nearby noise, like an electrical hum, can prevent them from focusing on anything else, and it will need to be removed before they can be expected to tune into people's voices.

Smell
This sense can easily be disregarded. Children with ASD have been known to identify people by their smell (looking at faces may be too difficult) and if someone changes their perfume or aftershave they may seem to be a 'new' person. Smells can be experienced as painful: one 6-year-old boy always went to the cloakroom corner at snack time and cried, shouted, stamped his feet and buried his head in someone's coat – the smell of crisps overwhelmed him and made him feel

sick. Once the problem was identified he was found somewhere else to sit and given something else to smell.

Taste

Children with ASD are frequently very particular about what they eat, often preferring a limited variety of food and sometimes smelling it before they eat. A 9-year-old in a special school, acting out a farmyard scene, instructed me to 'make the pig smell the horse, see if it smells safe'. Staff subsequently used this knowledge about his perception of 'safety' to help him gradually expand the variety of foods he was prepared to try.

Touch

Again, a sense that is sometimes neglected in its importance. Textures can be either greatly preferred and offer the child a degree of comfort, or else can be highly aversive. One 4-year-old boy ran over to a complete (and astonished) stranger so that he could have the pleasure of stroking the tights she was wearing. But a 9-year-old boy was so disturbed by the sensation created by the waistband of his uniform trousers that he regularly emerged from the toilets with his trousers round his ankles rather than do them up again. A pair of black jogging pants solved the problem and protected his dignity.

4

Teaching Approaches: Differentiating Work

'Don't tell me, show me!'

It is accepted good teaching practice to utilize pupils' strengths in order to support the development of their weaker abilities. This chapter will be emphasizing one of the common strengths of people with ASD – that of superior *visual* skill compared with other skills, including, and particularly, auditory abilities. To paraphrase another well-known, catchy slogan, when considering how to help the pupil with ASD, think: 'Visual, Visual, Visual!'

We have already looked at the need not to overload the visual environment of pupils with ASD from a sensory point of view (see Chapter 3, pp. 51–2), but provided the level and use of visual input is appropriate to the needs of the individual pupil, then this is probably their best route for understanding, remembering and learning. Making these adaptations might seem daunting in terms of extra work involved for the classroom staff. But as before, when the strategies for modifying the physical space within the classroom were described, the methods for maximizing the pupil's visual environment should not add significantly to the teacher's or TA's workloads over the long term. If the pupil has access to an LSA, then setting the strategies up are likely to be an important part of her role. Once they are set up it is likely – once again – that they will also benefit other pupils in the class.

Providing visual support

What we all think about and say to each other occurs in extremely subtle and abstract ways, which most of us learn early in life and soon take completely for granted. The relationship between thought and spoken language is an immensely complex one, and is certainly beyond the scope of this book. But most people are fluent speakers, who find it fairly easy to follow the flow of conversation around them and effortlessly transform what they are thinking into speech. Although some of us are much more skilled than others at expressing ourselves, most of us at least get by and can follow and convey meaning without difficulty.

For people with ASD, however, this may be a difficult process. Temple Grandin (1995), for example (she was quoted in Chapter 1, p. 13), has revealed that she tends to think in a series of pictures, and can prompt herself to remember a past event by, as it were, 'rewinding a video'. Spoken language is not, for her, an automatic form of communication, and speech is 'rapid' – it is here one moment and gone the next! The same is true for sign language and natural gesture. Oliver Sacks (1995) describes the difficulties Dr Grandin has as if she were an anthropologist from Mars needing to 'study' and analyse these 'strange beings' (i.e. us). There will be more detail on this topic in Chapter 5.

So if, as many people with ASD do, you find it difficult to 'tune into' people's speech, *and* your processing speed is slower than the average person's, *and*
your chances of getting a replay are minimal, then you
are likely, very quickly, to lose the 'thread' of a conversation and become confused. *And* it may be embar-
rassing (or impossible) to ask someone to repeat
themselves. But if what they are telling you (for
example: what to do, where to go, how to do something) is presented in visual form, however, then you
can look at it for as long as you need, or for as many
times as necessary, and it is present as a constant
reminder. Some examples of this type of visual guidance are given below. As before, the list is not definitive and there are many ways of providing this type of
support. First, however, it is necessary to look at the
level of understanding the child may have achieved.

Visual understanding: levels and aspects of understanding

The aspects of development outlined below relate only
to the purpose of this chapter and the strategies
described in it. They are not separate aspects of development because, of course, in 'real' children they
merge and overlap. They are described separately,
however, in order to clarify the different levels of need;
and the particular learning styles of children with ASD
are included in each point.

1. The child's development may have remained at an
   early stage (this may also be called the **pre-verbal**,
   or **pre-linguistic** stage) where they neither under-

stand nor use spoken language reliably. At this level, however, there may be some understanding of the **meaning of objects**: for example, when they see their usual cup appear they may know that a drink is on its way. Objects used in this way to support a child's understanding are usually referred to as '**objects of reference**'. Be aware, however, that children with ASD tend to have idiosyncratic ways of relating to objects. For example, a red jumper worn by Dad on one trip to the seaside may in the future be indelibly associated with the seaside. If Dad then wears that same jumper on a trip to the zoo the child may become 'inexplicably' confused and distressed!

2. The child may begin to understand and use very familiar aspects of language, such as their own name. This understanding is probably heavily dependent on the context ('Go and get your coat' may be 'understood' because Mum already has the car keys and a shopping bag). This should not mislead people into believing that the child's understanding is more reliable than it really is. Children with ASD often do not learn in the same way that other children do:

   ♦ they may know 'cup' – but only the green, plastic double-handled one they drink out of; to them, your coffee cup is not a cup;

   ♦ they may know the names of some dinosaurs, but not know the names of the other children in their class.

3. The child's understanding of the **words for objects** gradually becomes more reliable, and familiar words such as 'drink' and 'bath' are likely to be learned

more quickly than words that are without importance or heard less often, like 'pencil' or 'cabbage'. Words for things usually come first, and words for **actions**, **descriptions** (e.g. size, colour) and **ideas** or concepts (e.g. on/in/under, mine/his), and so on generally come later. For children with ASD, words for concrete objects are obviously much easier than abstract nouns (e.g. fear, beauty) or words that are relative (behind versus in front of – it all depends where you are standing).

4. The child may begin to show a preference for certain **pictures**, for example, family photos and simple drawings in books. The clearer the picture or photo, and the less background detail, the better for children with ASD. But remain aware that the child's interpretation of, or focus on, a picture may be very different from yours (remember the theory of central coherence). At this stage, the child may be able to learn a limited range of consistently used computer-generated 'symbols' (see p. 60–1).

5. A child with ASD learning to **read** is a topic that deserves a book all to itself. Some children with ASD do sometimes seem to 'acquire' the early ability to decode print, but do not assume they can understand what they are reading. This ability should be assessed as necessary.

6. A pupil's language and reading skills may appear to be age appropriate in all respects. For many pupils this assumption is understandable, but in ASD subtle and even significant problems can be missed (remember the 'spiky' profile referred to in Chapter 1). The language and reading skills of all pupils with

ASD should be assessed appropriately. Visual support is probably still necessary.

Visual timetables

Once you have established the stage the child has achieved (i.e. objects of reference, photos/pictures, pictures + words, words only – liaison with the SLT might help you establish this) then you can choose the appropriate method of visual support. Listed below are several ways of **informing** the child about what you want him to do, or what is going to happen. (Do not confuse these methods with PECS (mentioned in Chapters 5 and 7, pp. 69 and 97) which develops the child's ability to *express* himself.) Only a thorough knowledge of the child will help you decide which will suit him best. For detailed information on this type of support and use of structure, refer to the TEACCH contacts given in Chapter 7.

There are computer programmes for generating the type of picture symbols that can be used at this level. Some of these are listed in Chapter 7, p. 98.

Activity 1

Think about a child you know that has ASD. Using the guidelines above, try and work out the level his understanding has reached.

Before you continue with this chapter, devise a visual method to help him, for example, follow his morning routine from arrival at school to mid-morning break.

Some commonly used methods are described here. Since it is difficult to describe them fully, and for you to imagine them in use, it is also strongly recommended that you discuss the choice of method with a suitably qualified professional.

♦ *One at a time*: show the child the object (or photo) you have chosen to represent the activity about to take place. For example, show the child a paint brush to show that they are going to do some artwork, or a piece of seatbelt webbing to show they are going in the car/minibus (this is what the child *experiences*: a toy car may not mean anything!).

♦ *Key ring*: if you are using photos/pictures (or even small objects) then keeping a selection on a belt-loop key ring might be helpful, for example, 'toilet', 'sit down', 'listen'.

♦ *First, and then*: prepare a piece of A4 paper (laminated), divide it into two squares, and place an object picture/photo on each square to show the child that he is doing this **first**, **then** that. The second object or picture might be the child's reward for having completed the first task. Use a small piece of Velcro, one half glued to the centre of each area and the corresponding half onto the picture/object, to keep them in place.

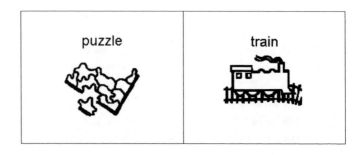

♦ *Series of pictures or photos*: if the child is ready for a short series (no more than two or three to begin with) then he is probably able to use pictures rather than objects. This is a big step: it is crucial to go slowly and build on previous success.

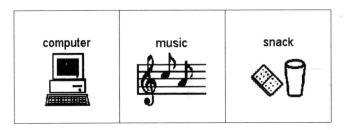

♦ *A written list*: this is a huge leap, from a picture series to a written list! Again, advice and consultation is vital and building upon the child's successes and confidence – in other words, knowing the child and what they are ready for is crucial. For example:

✓ quiet reading time

✓ register

✓ assembly

✓ literacy hour

✓ finish off yesterday's work

✓ snack

✓ break

There are several points to remember, whatever age the pupil, or whichever method you choose, and these are listed briefly below.

1. As each activity is completed, the object or picture must be removed, or the word crossed out – whatever suits the child to convey 'finished'. A tip: have, for example, a 'Monday' envelope, and so on, with pictures/lists duplicated throughout the week as needed, so that you are not constantly hunting for what you need.

2. Most people seem to choose a left → right, horizontal orientation to display the pictures. Displaying them vertically (top → bottom) is fine too, just as long as you are always consistent.

3. Position the objects or pictures where they are most convenient for the child to see and understand them. This may sound obvious, but I have often seen them placed too high, or on a wall that the child does not ever look at. Only use as many as the child needs (or can cope with) at a time: I have seen special school classroom walls unhelpfully festooned with the whole week's timetable!

4. Whatever method you choose, and whatever you select to represent an activity must remain consistent. A child using a brush for art in one class then being shown an apron in the next class will be confused at best, and possibly quite distressed. In special educational settings it is worth appointing someone to ensure that this consistency is maintained throughout the school.

5. Introduce some way of depicting (a) 'choose' for times when the child can choose his own activity, and (b) 'change' for when unavoidable change occurs (see also Chapter 6). Show him, 'Look,

Daniel, no outdoor play today (place 'change' symbol over the one for outdoor play), we're going into the hall' (substitute the picture, or photo, of 'hall').

Visual structure

Many pupils with ASD can become quite distressed by being presented with a blank sheet of paper to 'write about . . .'. Creating ideas from nothing is very difficult for them (think back to some of the problems outlined in the psychological theories, executive dysfunction particularly). There are many simple methods of providing clear visual guidance so that pupils can see what is expected of them and how to go about it. The following suggestions also show how work can be differentiated to the standard the child can be expected to achieve, with some comments on expectations toward the end.

♦ *'Here's one I made earlier!'* A familiar phrase to many of us, I'm sure, and what has worked for television audiences over the years has often worked for children with ASD. If you want them to make, for example, a model of something, have one ready to show them what it is they need to do.

♦ *Boxes and numbers*: The 'blank sheet of paper' I referred to above can be transformed by a range of quick and straightforward ways. For example, (a) to draw a picture of something, provide a box in which to draw it:

or (b) to write a story, provide numbered boxes with prompts:

1. **Who** is the story about?
2. **Where** did they go?
3. **What** did they do?
4. **How** did the story end?

♦ *Lists*: Similar to the section on timetables, the use of picture charts or written lists of what is going to happen today can be made to show (a) the equipment that is needed to do the task, and (b) each of the steps necessary to carry out the task. Part of the TA's or LSA's role may be to help with this. Older pupils might be encouraged to devise and develop their own lists; they will clearly need a lot of help to do this initially, but with practice they can use this method to become more organized and independent.

♦ *Worksheets*: Disliked, even disapproved of, by some people, worksheets are often a great help to children with ASD. They tend to set work out in a way that they understand, showing clearly (a) how much they need to do, (b) what to do, and (c) evidence of completion. This 'closed' style of working can also be adapted for use in many other ways.

Realistic expectations

It is important for all teachers to have sufficient understanding of their pupils' abilities upon which to base expectations; this is also true of children with ASD. However, where addressing other reasons for underachievement, such as emotional and behavioural problems, or difficulties listening and attending, might result in a child performing nearer to their own potential, this is not necessarily the case with a child with ASD. Providing practical support for the child, as suggested throughout this book, should help the child to feel more confident and help him to access the curriculum. But where his ASD is considered to be severely affecting his access to the curriculum it may be that setting realistic aims to help him achieve his (and the teacher's) best is quite sufficient.

If the pupil appears to be cognitively very able, perceived underachievement can be frustrating for parents and teachers alike. It must be emphasized, however, that realistic expectations of what the child can achieve are essential for his confidence and self-esteem: a little work, carried out well, for example, can and should be praised appropriately. **It is quite acceptable for the child not to succeed, at the level of his potential, all the time.**

Rewards and 'time to be autistic'

In line with the introduction of an appropriate reward system, and setting realistic expectations, it is of great importance to recognize the pupil's ASD by allowing time within his school day to 'be autistic'. We all have our own ways of relaxing and allowing daily stresses to recede. Most of us can wait until we get home to, for example, curl up on the sofa, watch a soap opera and drink a glass of red wine. But remember the comparison made by Oliver Sacks: for a person with ASD their day may be akin to a constant intellectual analysis of every moment and nuance of people's behaviour, and the stresses upon them are likely to be far greater. For younger children with ASD playtime is not the relaxing period it is for the others, it can be hard work and stressful. For teenagers with ASD, there may be additional worries about their status and acceptance, and high levels of anxiety are common.

At some point in their school day, the child with ASD will probably need to go and exercise their own particular special interest or behaviour. This may vary from standing in the corner of the playground, rocking to and fro and flicking their fingers, to reading through their collection of fire extinguisher serial numbers. But whatever it is, a quiet place to do it, free from the potential misunderstanding of others, is crucial.

In introducing an appropriate reward system, it is quite feasible to make limited use of a child's interests and obsessions as a reward – time and place are the important points here. Indeed, allowing five minutes at the end of work to go and drive Thomas the Tank Engine around his track may not only reduce anxiety but also act as motivation for completing a task. Interests and obsessions can be managed in this way to prevent them from interfering and distracting the child at times when he does need to be working. Do involve the child's parents in discussion about the most appropriate reward system and who confers the rewards.

5

Teaching Approaches: Language, Communication and Social Skills

Before language

As noted in the previous chapter, the flow of language most of us use appears effortless, and the skills that underpin and accompany language development are also taken largely for granted. I want to start this chapter by looking, very briefly, at some of those skills.

Attention and listening

These abilities have received a good deal of coverage lately, with, for example, 'Sure Start' emphasizing the need for parents to play with their babies and turn the television off so that speech can be heard. Without the ability to listen to and 'tune into' language, for whatever reason, development may be delayed. Children with autism, as we've seen, find it difficult to share attention with someone else and listen to people talking.

Play

The development of play and language are closely associated; there is not space here to explain this, but

Chapter 7 contains some book titles that the interested reader may like to refer to. As we've seen, the play skills of children with ASD are often disordered. This can vary: imaginative, pretend and symbolic play might fail to develop at all, the child preferring, for example, to spin the wheels of a truck rather than 'brrooom' it along. Or the child might appear to play imaginatively, acting out parts from favourite videos, but without adding ideas of his own or allowing anyone else to join in.

Communication

Long before language appears in the form of words, around the end of the first year, a normally developing baby is able to communicate astonishingly effectively. The taking turns in a two-way 'dance', that begins with the tiny baby smiling, starts a life-long process of taking turns in 'conversation'. As adults we interpret babies' sounds and actions, endowing them with meaning, and gradually they start to understand that they, too, can intentionally communicate their needs and share interests with us. Retrospectively, it is often realized that babies who go on to be diagnosed with ASD have not developed the usual communication patterns. Parents frequently use phrases such as, 'He was never really "with us"'. Again, please refer to Chapter 7 for titles of books that describe these processes in more detail.

The language styles of children with ASD

Fundamental to the language development of children with ASD is how they *use* language to communicate: this will be covered in more detail later in the chapter.

First, however, I wish to look briefly at the language profiles that are common among children with ASD. SLTs usually assess the following language areas:

♦ the words they know (receptive vocabulary and concept knowledge, such as size, place, e.g. on/under);

♦ the flow of language (including instructions, questions) they can understand (receptive language);

♦ the words they can recall and use (expressive vocabulary and concept use);

♦ the sentences and narrative they can construct (expressive language), including their use of grammar (e.g. '-ed' word endings to denote the past; pronouns).

Language profiles

Many children with ASD, particularly those with accompanying learning difficulties, do not develop spoken language. This may be because their abilities do not progress beyond the developmental stage where language development would occur (refer back to Chapter 4, where pre-verbal or pre-linguistic skills were discussed, p. 56). They may, however, be able to understand some of what is said to them, but without being able to formulate their own responses (i.e. they are non-verbal). To aid the spontaneous expressive skills of these children, the use of the Picture Exchange Communication System (PECS), building on their visual strengths, has transformed the lives of many of these children.

Teachers of children with limited expressive language skills should familiarize themselves with this system.

Children with ASD may develop spoken language with varying degrees of skill. They may be able to voice their wishes and basic needs, but without seeing any point in commenting on, for example, an animal in a field. Conversation with these children can feel like hard work, with the adult supplying all the suggestions and content while the child answers in single words. Alternatively, they may acquire a sophisticated vocabulary and be able to talk at great length (like Daniel and James), sounding fluent but without the ability to sustain a conversation.

Several characteristics are common in the language of these children.

♦ Difficulty processing what has been said to them because (a) it was too long, (b) it contained too many relative concepts (e.g. size contrasts such as bigger/smaller), (c) it was about something abstract and not about the 'here and now' (e.g. 'What did you do at the weekend?'), and (d) it was said too quickly.

♦ Some children, particularly those with learning difficulties, may repeat back what has just been said (this is called echolalia) in an effort to process it, and to show that they are willing to respond – they just don't know how to.

♦ The apparent fluency of their expressive language masks both their limited processing skills and their difficulty with *reciprocating* – i.e. having a two-way conversation.

♦ A tendency to use either a 'flat' tone or an exaggeratedly 'sing-song' voice.

♦ A marked tendency to take things literally: one teacher was surprised to see a boy (and his book) disappear from the room after being told to, 'Go to your drawer and take your book out'.

Activity 1

Think of a child with ASD that you know and, using the information above, try and construct a language profile for him. If the child has an SLT then compare your profile with his/hers.

Given the child's particular profile, what difficulties do you think he might have in the classroom?

Language for learning

During Key Stage 1, it is assumed that all children are still learning language. In mainstream schools, from Key Stage 2 onwards, it is assumed that their language is proficient and can support their learning. That is, they can use language functionally to, for example, give descriptions and explanations; define words; make comparisons and links between cause and effect; and solve everyday problems. They are beginning to master skills such as interpretation and inference.

It is probable that children with ASD, reaching Key Stage 2, are still learning many of the basic language skills that their peers have grasped intuitively, and that the more subtle, higher level language skills needed for interpretation and inference will remain extremely difficult for them. As the other children use their language as a base for future learning, children with ASD begin to get left behind.

What, then, can you do to help the child with ASD?

The next section deals with some of the strategies that you can use to enhance their language understanding and use.

The language styles of teachers

Watch your language!

Some years ago I was cycling in Holland on my own, with an inadequate map, and I got lost. Knowing that if I could just find my way back to a village called Elspeet I could retrace my steps, I asked someone, '*Elspeet, alstublieft* (please)?' He went into a long, rapid explanation – the only word of which I picked out was, '*Links* (left)'. What could it mean? Turn second left? Turn right, then left? Without a context, one word meant nothing and I remained lost. This is what language often feels like for children with ASD – a rapid, foreign language that they struggle to understand. Below are some suggestions to help the child with ASD understand you.

♦ Face the pupil and start the instruction with his name (there is no necessity to make, or insist, on eye-contact – a listening posture is sufficient). 'Joshua, sit down,' sounds blunt, but usually works well.

♦ Break up what you need to say: three short instructions, with pauses between them, are better than one long one.

♦ Speak more slowly and give the pupil time to process what you have said; this may mean waiting what, for us, would be an uncomfortable length of time. It's only you who is uncomfortable!

♦ Monitor your use of vocabulary: a pupil told to, 'Go and stand on the *far side*,' might have no idea where you mean.

Say what you mean and mean what you say

Metaphor, idiom and sarcasm are usually lost on pupils with ASD. One 10-year-old, when the class was told that the last person to finish would have his head cut off, rushed his work in such a panic he then found himself in trouble for messy work. A 4-year-old, asked to, 'Come here, "sausage,"' looked around him solemnly and replied that he didn't have one.

Asking a pupil politely, 'Would you like to . . .?' may result in the blunt response, 'No'. Try to monitor your own language so that if the pupil reacts oddly – or, apparently, defiantly – think back about what you've just said. This might be difficult to do initially, because we say such things all the time without realizing.

Pupils can learn what idioms mean, but may have to do so one at a time. One high school pupil made himself a book of sayings and their meanings, illustrated with little cartoon characters.

To repeat or not to repeat

With most children, if we think they have not understood us, we rephrase what we have said. For children with ASD, who are trying to process what you said first, they are likely to think that you have said something completely different, and will go to the beginning to start all over again. So, first,

♦ pause; wait to see if he has understood.

Then, if you think he has not understood:

♦ tell him, 'Adam, I'm going to say it another way' and then rephrase;

♦ if necessary, break up or shorten what you've said;

♦ replace the word(s) that might have confused him.

Again, teachers often worry about the other children in the class – your remit, after all, is to stimulate their language! But the use of clear, concise and unambiguous language often benefits many of the other children; and the habit of telling the whole class first and then adding a modified version for the child with ASD, does develop quite quickly.

Communication and social skills

This area, perhaps more than any other, characterizes the most significant difficulties experienced by people with ASD. While, again, they can often learn and adapt to 'our' world they will always have difficulties generalizing what they have learnt and may have to learn afresh for almost every new situation they encounter.

We use our communication skills to develop, sustain and regulate our social relationships. Although many people with ASD do prefer to remain apart from social contact, for others the drive toward socialization may be as important as it is for anyone else, and the need for acceptance and approval just as strong. Their sense of failure and isolation may then be powerful and the anxiety and exhaustion caused by the need for constant effort must never be underestimated.

The range of social communication difficulties

People with ASD are prone to have some, or even all of the difficulties listed below.

♦ Difficulties with understanding and using all non-verbal forms of communication, for example, gesture, body language, personal space, and, particularly, facial expressions.

♦ As already noted, limited knowledge of conversational 'rules', particularly its two-way nature.

♦ Limited understanding of their own and other people's feelings and emotions; very restricted empathy skills, which can make them appear blunt or thoughtless.

♦ Limited understanding of the 'short-hand' that we use in everyday social contact. For example, 'Can you put the book down?' → 'Yes'.

♦ Understanding that we use different styles to talk to different people: chatting in the familiar way appropriate with your peers does not go down well with the headteacher.

♦ Their own idiosyncratic way of communicating and dealing with social encounters, for example, beginning a conversation by kicking someone, abruptly saying 'goodbye' and walking off, or insisting on standing against a wall to talk to someone.

♦ Needing to manage sensory overload during conversation, for example, little/no eye-contact, rocking or flapping their fingers/hands.

People with ASD can appear socially awkward and naïve. Think of Mr Bean and Frank Spencer (widely believed to have forms of ASD), and their respective difficulties fitting in with the social norms and expectations most of us understand intuitively.

How can we help?

♦ It is absolutely vital that when social skills are taught, they are linked firmly to their context (see Chapter 6, 'Social skills' pp 89–90). If skills are taught elsewhere (such as a clinic setting) then they must be transferred to the appropriate context.

♦ The skills that are taught should be of importance to the pupil's everyday life (don't just teach something because it is on a checklist); it is essential that he understands the need and importance of what he is learning.

♦ Skills can be taught on an individual basis (again, see Chapter 6, 'Social skills') and then transferred to a group setting as and when necessary.

♦ It may be possible to model social skills, and good peer role models can be particularly helpful (see 'Circle of Friends', below, p. 79). But, remember that pupils with ASD tend not to learn incidentally and they will probably need to practise what they do learn in each new context.

Activity 2
Think of one particular difficulty experienced by someone you know with ASD. Does it appear on the list above? How does it affect the life of that person?

Can you think of some practical strategies that might help him with that one difficulty?

This might be best done as a shared or group activity.

Problems → activities

It is only possible here to explore a few of the problems experienced by people with ASD, with a sample of strategies, materials and resources that might be useful. All these activities can be adapted for use in mainstream or special educational settings.

First, activities targeting particular difficulties. (There are obviously many other ways to develop these same skills.)

Focus: listening to other people

Activity: In an even numbered group put the pupils in pairs. Give them a list of three things to find out about each other (e.g. favourite TV programme). Give them a few minutes to talk to each other. Ask the pupils to recall what the *other* person's favourite things were. How well did they listen to each other? Practise accordingly.

Focus: how much space?

Activity: Again in pairs, give each a sheet of broad-sheet newspaper and ask them to spread it out. Tell them to stand either side of the paper and encourage some discussion about whether this is a comfortable distance to stand next to someone. Then ask them to fold the piece of paper in half, and in half again, each time exploring how *uncomfortable* this becomes, and why. Explain that by remembering the size of the piece of paper they can judge how close to stand to people in social situations. For younger children you could turn this into 'Musical newspapers'. (But remind them never to take a piece of paper with them to social occasions!)

Focus: how to interrupt appropriately
Activity: While pupils with ASD watch, three adults role-play two scenes. First, two people are interrupted by a third in a rude and inappropriate way. Talk about the scene and what went wrong. Second, use the methods that have been discussed to demonstrate appropriate ways to interrupt. Using a camcorder for comparison is useful here.

Focus: emotion vocabulary
Activity: Something has just occurred that has created high levels of emotion, for example, a playground incident or the death of someone's pet. Individually or in a small group, explore some of the words that we use to describe a particular emotion (e.g. anger → annoyed, cross, mad, furious, in a rage); help the pupils to rank the strength of these emotions on a scale of 1 to 5 (using, for example, an emotion ladder, thermometer). Go back to the incident and see where each of them would place it in terms of the scale you have all created.

Second, here is a list of useful resources that might help to develop different aspects of social skills.

1. *Ready-made social skills programmes and activities.* There are a great many of these available now and a thorough search will help you to decide which might be useful for your pupils. Two are listed here:

- *Social Skills Programmes* by Maureen Aarons and Tessa Gittens (2003);

- *Talkabout* by Alex Kelly.

2. *Mind Reading.* This CD-ROM and DVD has been designed to help pupils learn to recognize and interpret facial expressions, voices and behaviour. (See p. 99 for more detail.)

3. *Social Stories.* A method of fostering social understanding developed by Carol Gray (see p. 98), this gently helps (and reminds) pupils to understand the need for certain social behaviours, such as lining up or not indulging in unpleasant personal habits.

4. *Circle of Friends.* This is a programme that recruits the understanding and support of other pupils in a class, and provides them with knowledge about the social difficulties experienced by their classmate with ASD (see p. 98 for the details). There are also less formal ways of doing this, which might be loosely termed a 'buddy system'. This enlists the support of a group of pupils to look out for the problems that ASD pupils (particularly at high school) might experience, such as getting from one class to the next, and bullying. Always gain the permission of the pupil and/or his parents before embarking on this type of system. Never place the responsibility on just one pupil, however socially able and respected – all teenagers have their own image to consider.

These are just some of the ideas and resources that are available (see Chapter 7 for details of more); a glance through a range of publishers' catalogues will demonstrate some of the ways these needs can be addressed.

The role of the speech and language therapist

Anyone familiar with the ASD work carried out by speech and language therapists (SLTs) may know that, while they do not usually assess 'speech', they do investigate and assess language and communication abilities, and access to an SLT with specialist knowledge of ASD is crucial. My own experiences suggest that it is all too easy to make assumptions about the language abilities of pupils with ASD, and only thorough assessment will reveal the extent of their needs. In addition, the interface between language and communication that underpins all their educational and social skills, makes multi-disciplinary working essential.

The SLT may be able to come into school to work with the child directly; this is often not the case, however, given the numbers of children with ASD and the national shortage of SLTs. It may also not be necessary, as the SLT can liaise closely with the teacher and work effectively by training others (particularly the LSA or TA) to carry out programmes of work, or target particular areas of social difficulty. This way the language and communication needs of the pupil are met and generalized throughout his school day and not just during his half-hour with the SLT.

6

Managing Change

Flexibility in a safe environment

It has already been noted that people with ASD experience difficulty dealing with change of many kinds, whether it is the layout in the classroom (or supermarket), or a change to the usual timetable. Chapter 3 and Chapter 4 (Visual timetable, p. 59) describe how to prepare pupils for change using visual methods. But since there are many potential changes during a school day, some long-term strategies for coping with them might be helpful. While difficulty being flexible is typical in ASD, developing pupils' ability to cope with change is key to reducing their anxiety.

Coping with change

Families often describe how their children insist on using the same route to get to, for example, Granny's; and how, if they go another way or if they go somewhere else using that same route, there may be panic and tears. In school I have often watched children become distressed if something is done a different way. In one extreme case, a boy was unable to settle or comply for an entire morning – until someone realized that the birdseed in the classroom's budgie cage was not hanging in its usual place.

Some strategies for helping these children to deal with change are listed below; as before, many of them use visual means.

♦ If they are able to see change occurring, then that will often go a long way to helping them accept it: show them that the pencils were kept *there*, now they are *here*.

♦ If possible, change only one thing at a time: finding the pencils in their new place can be managed; finding several other things in new locations might result in overload (see Chapter 3, p. 41).

♦ As described in Chapter 4, use the visual timetable to show them when changes to the school routine are going to take place.

♦ Use pictures, diagrams and maps. If, for example, there are roadworks necessitating a change of route to school, show them on a map, or through role-play, where their house and the school are, with appropriate landmarks added so that they can look out for them.

♦ If a regular supply teacher is going to take the class, ask him or her if they are happy to provide a photo so that the pupil knows who is coming; and don't assume they can remember the new teacher's name. If supply teachers are usually unknown, have a general picture or symbol for 'supply teacher' (refer back to Chapter 4, and to Chapter 7 for details of computer-generated symbols). It is also worth mentioning here that much of what unsettles the pupil with ASD when a supply teacher takes the class are the changes in the behaviour of the other pupils!

♦ If the teacher is planning, for example, a new hair-style (or beard removal), take 'before and after' photos, wearing the same clothes in both pictures. If possible discuss the planned change beforehand, using the photos once the change has been made.

I've started so I'll finish

In contrast to the suggestions above, it is often better to let a pupil finish whatever he has begun. Leaving a piece of work, once started, may be quite intolerable for him. Ensure that you have allowed time for him to finish. Similarly, if you have asked him to do three things, don't try and squeeze a fourth in: that's the deal!

Perfection

A form of 'sameness' for many pupils with ASD is the need to achieve perfection in, for example, their written work. While this sounds quite reasonable at first glance, it can be highly disabling and a cause of considerable distress, as the pen portrait below demonstrates.

For Thomas, just writing the date and the title of his piece of work represented a daily crisis, striving as he did to do it to his own standard of satisfaction. Perceiving his efforts to be less than perfect he rubbed out what he'd written, so now the page was grubby. Repeated attempts ended in the page tearing. This page was discarded and Thomas had another go, only for the same to happen but with growing anxiety. The other pupils would complete their work before Thomas had begun.

If he did manage to complete the date and title, then further problems emerged. In Years 1 and 2 he found number work easier than literacy work and usually got all his sums right. But by Year 3 he began to struggle with some of the language concepts involved. He then found that the teacher returned his work with 'red writing' and sometimes crosses on it instead of ticks. This made him feel terribly anxious and also angry. One day he shouted at the teacher and told her not to write on his work.

Thomas's teacher discussed these difficulties with his mother and the SLT. It was agreed that:

♦ He would be shown some of the other children's attempts, complete with corrections, with which to compare his own.

♦ He could have only two attempts at writing the date and the title; after that he must get on with his work. This 'rule' was written down on a piece of laminated card and taped to the corner of his desk.

♦ A Social Story (see Chapter 5, p. 79) would be written to help Thomas understand that it is OK to make mistakes and that this is one way the teacher can help him to learn.

Keeping some things the same

Deciding which things to change and what to keep the same will, as with so many other aspects of ASD, depend on the needs of the individual child; there is no substitute for a thorough knowledge of what those needs are. There is sometimes a tendency to see the need to maintain sameness in certain aspects of school life as 'giving in' to the child and his ASD. This is not the case, any more than making provision for wheelchair users, or for children with a hearing impairment, is 'giving in' to individual 'whims'.

In managing change and developing a more flexible approach to life, it will be necessary to ensure that other parts of the school day hold no surprises. If, after managing to sit through a theatre company's production in the school hall, he then wants to return to his usual place in class, eat the contents of his lunchbox in exactly the same order as yesterday, and talk to nobody, then he should know in advance that those needs will be accommodated.

Transitions: starting or changing school

One of the most anxious times for both parents and pupils is when the child starts attending a school at school entry, or transfers to the next Key Stage. The transition to high school is probably the most anxious time of all, as it involves a much bigger building, as well as regular changes of teacher and classroom. There is a great deal that can be done to prepare the child for these changes in their routine. Again, whenever possible, do involve the parents in the preparations for the transfer from one school to the next.

Getting to know the school

♦ Most pupils will have the opportunity to look at their new school, but discuss with staff there the possibility of some **extra visits**. Initially, these visits could be made while the other pupils are in class so he can look round while there is no additional noise or bustle. If a primary school-aged child has an LSA then she might be able to take him, and one or two other children who would also benefit.

♦ On these visits, **identify key places** within the new setting, for example, the toilets, dining area, and a 'safe haven' (see below, 'Social skills', p. 89).

♦ Take a digital camera and take some photos of the building and of significant features. Use these to compile a personalized **photo book** that the child can look at when talking about transferring to the new school.

♦ The photo book could begin with a **map of the school** showing where each of the photos has been taken. Where appropriate, this might also show the route to school.

♦ Compile a collection of **facts about the school** that will be relevant to the pupil; but do be careful not to overload him in the early stages. For example, establishing what the uniform consists of, including the PE requirements, would be necessary. At Key Stages 3 and 4, ask to look at a sample timetable, showing the changes of room and teacher; the subjects could be colour-coded for 'at a glance' identification.

◆ A child attending school for the first time might be able to meet his teacher before the start of term. If the school staff are willing, **photographs** might be obtained so that the pupil knows who his teacher(s) and midday assistants will be.

Getting to know the pupil

◆ A **pen portrait** of the pupil, briefly outlining his likes/dislikes, learning and social styles would be useful for the new teacher(s). If appropriate, he could contribute to this himself.

◆ Set up a consistent method of communication between school and home, for example, a **home–school diary**. This should record positive and praise-worthy news as well as reasons for concern.

◆ Whenever possible, **a visit** from the new staff to the pupil's current school will be helpful, so that they can see him in context, both in terms of his learning and his ability to relate to other people, particularly the other children. This is particularly important for the staff who might be supporting the pupil at his new school.

◆ If necessary, identify (and provide information for) the **key people** who will be supporting the pupil at school and in the playground, for example, a TA, LSA, or midday assistant. Don't leave it until some-thing happens before identifying the people who will need to deal with difficult situations.

◆ Whenever possible arrange **whole-school training** in ASD. This may be carried out before the pupil arrives at the school, although it may be more useful once the pupil has been at the school three to four weeks and the staff have been able to get to know him a little. If, from discussion and visits to the pupil's current school, it emerges that there may be difficulties then prior knowledge and understanding is preferable.

New routines

The following suggestions constitute a list of possibilities. Many of the suggestions are particular to high school, and a book called *The Big School* (Maines and Robinson, 1997) might be useful. Discussions with parents, staff and professionals should give some guidance as to which of the ideas are needed.

♦ Designate a **key person** and a **room** with time set aside daily so that the pupil can be informed of changes and homework requirements. Homework is, after all, *school* work and a lot of pupils with ASD experience great difficulty with this concept. Many schools now have homework clubs so that they can complete work in the school setting. They are likely to need additional help recording what they are expected to do.

♦ Arrange for support at the **beginning and end of each lesson**, particularly moving from one lesson to the next. The 'buddy system' outlined in Chapter 5 (p. 79) might help with this.

♦ Provide support during – or possibly alternative arrangements for – **breaks and lunchtimes** (see Chapter 3, p. 48).

- Practise using the **new route** to school or, if the pupil does not go independently to school, practise the new drop-off and collection arrangements.

- Make **equipment lists** for each lesson.

- Make a **list** of what to pack for each day.

- Make a pocket-sized **timetable**, laminated and colour-coded.

- Do not assume that, because the pupil knew how to do something in one school (or at home), he will be able to carry that knowledge over to the new school: he may need to **re-learn skills** in the new context.

Social skills

Attention to all or most of the following points is essential, as emotional well-being and security are an important basis for effective learning.

- Provision of a **safe-haven** during school hours. This can be, for example, the library if the pupil is relatively independent. Other arrangements may be necessary (e.g. quiet corner of the classroom, computer room, learning centre) where supervision is required.

- Find an alternative **place to eat lunch** if necessary; again, supervision is needed.

- Provision of opportunities for the pupil to **relax and socialize safely**, and without fear of bullying, with his peers. Develop peer support where possible: being seen in the company of adults and particularly an LSA (who is often female) is not 'cool', particularly when the pupil is craving the company of his peers.

♦ As noted previously, provision of a daily method for the pupil to **off-load anxieties** and to 'unpick' the day's events is important. This is also a relevant way of teaching the skills needed (along with the accompanying emotional aspects) to be able to socialize successfully. The person providing this support may also be able to act as an 'interpreter', hearing the pupil's own perspective, when things have gone wrong.

And finally . . .

While understanding that the pupil with ASD may be anxious about, and daunted by, school life at all levels, and by change in particular, implementing proactive strategies and enabling him to cope as positively as possible will help him gain confidence – and will mean that he copes better in the future. A positive cycle has been established!

7

Information and Resources

Support groups and information

The National Autistic Society
393 City Road, London EC1V 1NG
Tel.: 020 7903 3595
Fax: 020 7833 9666
Autism Helpline: 0845 070 4004
Website: www.nas.org.uk

The **National Autism Plan for Children** (**NAP-C**) is the work of **NIASA** (National Initiative: Autism Screening and Assessment), a core group of experts in ASD, promoting good working practices nationally. Typing 'National Autism Plan for Children' into a search engine should bring up this document. It can also be found on: www.cafamily.org.uk/campaigns.html

Autistic Spectrum Disorders: Good Practice Guidance
Available from: DfES Publications, PO Box 5050, Sherwood Park, Annesley, Nottingham NG15 0DJ
Tel.: 0845 602 2260
Fax: 0845 603 3360
Website: www.dfes.gov.uk/sen quote: DfES/579/2002
also http://inclusion.ngfl.gov.uk

ASD and Numeracy
As above but quote DfES/0511/2001 instead.

Autism Independent UK (including information on TEACCH training)
SFTAH, 199–203 Blandford Avenue, Kettering, Northants. NN16 9AT
Tel./Fax: 01536 523 274
Website: www.autismuk.com

Websites

www.aboutautism.org.uk: a parent's perspective.
www.skill.org.uk: not ASD-specific, but useful information for young people and adults with a disability.
www.myautis.com and www.myautis.com/famousas pies.html: an excellent site created by someone with Asperger's syndrome.
www.tonyattwood.com.au: a useful website for information and resources.

Book list (** next to a book denotes a detailed and in-depth text)

Attwood, T. (2000) *Asperger's Syndrome: A Guide for Parents and Professionals.* London: Jessica Kingsley.

Baron-Cohen, S. and Bolton, P. (2001) *Autism: The Facts.* Oxford: Oxford Medical Publications.

Bogdashina, O. (2005) *Communication Issues in Autism and Asperger Syndrome: Do We Speak the Same Language?* London: Jessica Kingsley.**

Clements, J. and Zarkowska, E. (2001) *Behavioural*

Concerns and Autistic Spectrum Disorders: Explanations and Strategies for Change. London: Jessica Kingsley.**

Cumine, V., Leach, J. and Stevenson, G. (1998) *Asperger Syndrome: A Practical Guide for Teachers.* London: David Fulton.

Cumine, V., Leach, J. and Stevenson, G. (2000) *Autism in the Early Years.* London: David Fulton.

Fleming, P., Miller, C. and Wright, J. (1997) *Speech and Language Difficulties In Education: Approaches to Collaborative Practice for Teachers and Speech and Language Therapists.* Bicester, Oxon: Speechmark.

Frith, U. (2003) *Autism: Explaining the Enigma* (2nd edn). Oxford: Blackwell.**

Gillberg, C. (2002) *A Guide to Asperger's Syndrome.* Cambridge: Cambridge University Press.**

Grandin, T. (1995) 'How people with autism think', in E. Schopler and G. Mesibov (eds) *Learning and Cognition in Autism.* New York: Plenum Press.

Haddon, M. (2003) *The Curious Incident of the Dog in the Night-Time.* London: Jonathan Cape.

Hesmondhalgh, M. and Breakey, C. (2001) *Access and Inclusion for Children with Autistic Spectrum Disorders: "Let Me In."* London: Jessica Kingsley.**

Hobson, P. (2002) *The Cradle of Thought: Exploring the Origins of Thinking.* London: Macmillan.**

Jackson, L. (2002) *Freaks, Geeks and Asperger's syndrome.* London: Jessica Kingsley.

Jordan, R. (1999) *Autistic Spectrum Disorder: An Introductory Handbook for Practitioners.* London: David Fulton.**

Jordan, R. (2001) *Autism with Severe Learning Difficulties.* London: Souvenir Press.**

Jordan, R. and Jones, G. (1999) *Meeting the Needs of Children with Autistic Spectrum Disorders.* London: David Fulton.**

Park, C.C. (1995) *The Siege: A Family's Journey into the World of an Autistic Child.* London: Little, Brown and Company.

Park, C.C. (2001) *Exiting Nirvana: A Daughter's Life with Autism.* London: Aurum Press.

Peeters, T. (1997) *Autism: From Theoretical Understanding to Educational Intervention.* London: Whurr.**

Sacks, O. (1995) *An Anthropologist From Mars.* London: Picador.

Sainsbury, C. (2000) *Martian in the Playground.* Bristol: Lucky Duck.

Sherratt, D. and Peter, M. (2002) *Developing Play and Drama in Children with Autistic Spectrum Disorder.* London: David Fulton.

Smith Myles, B., Tapscott Cook, K., Miller, N.E., Rinner, L. and Robbins, L.A. (2000) *Asperger Syndrome and Sensory Issues: Practical Solutions for Making Sense of the World.* Bicester, Oxon: Winslow.

Vermeulen, P. (2000) *I Am Special.* London: Jessica Kingsley.

Whittaker, P. (2001) *Challenging Behaviour and Autism: A Guide to Preventing and Managing Challenging Behaviour for Parents and Teachers.* London: NAS Publications.

Williams, D. (1992) *Nobody, Nowhere.* New York: Time Books.

Williams, D. (1994) *Somebody, Somewhere.* New York: Time Books.

Williams, D. (1996) *Autism: An Inside-Out Approach.*

London: Jessica Kingsley.

Wolfberg, P.J. (1999) *Play and Imagination in Children with Autism*. New York: Teachers College Press.**

Contacts

Ros Blackburn

Anyone wishing to contact Ros Blackburn in order to arrange a talk about living and working with autism can contact her via Dr Glenys Jones at the University of Birmingham. Email: g.e.jones@bham.ac.uk.

Richard Exley

Richard Exley's work is wide ranging and includes autism and Asperger's syndrome. He works with children, young people and adults with autism and with their families and siblings. He gives lectures and advises professionals in a range of settings including schools, hospitals and prisons. He can be contacted on richard exley@merseymail.com

Catalogues

The catalogues of the following publishers may in themselves be useful, as they contain many books and resources:

♦ Jessica Kingsley Publishers
   116 Pentonville Road, London N1 9JB
   Tel.: 020 7833 2307
   Website: www.jkp.com

♦ David Fulton
The Chiswick Centre, 414 Chiswick High Road, London W4 5TF
Tel.: 020 8996 3610
Website: www.fultonpublishers.co.uk

♦ Lucky Duck
Orders and customer services enquiries to:
SAGE Publications Ltd., 1 Oliver's Yard, 55 City Road, London EC1Y 1SP
Tel.: 020 7324 8500
Website: www.luckyduck.co.uk

♦ Speechmark
Telford Road, Bicester, Oxon OX26 4LQ
Tel.: 0186 924 4644
Website: www.speechmark.net

Diagnosis

♦ Diagnostic and Statistical Manual of Mental Disorders (**DSM-IV**) (4th edn) American Psychiatric Association (1994).

♦ International Classification of Diseases (**ICD-10**). *Mental Disorders: A glossary and guide to their classification with the 10th revision of the International Classification of Diseases*. (10th edn). World Health Organization (1993).

Assessments and checklists

Aarons, M. and Gittens, T. (1992) *The Autistic Continuum: An Assessment and Intervention*

Schedule. Windsor: NFER-Nelson.

Bishop, D.V.M. (2003) *The Children's Communication Checklist* (CCC-2) (2nd edn). London: The Psychological Corporation.

Dewart, H. and Summers, S. (1995) *The Pragmatic Profile of Everyday Communication Skills in Children.* Windsor: NFER-Nelson.

Gilliam, J.E. (1995) *The Gilliam Rating Scale* (GARS) Austin, Texas: Pro-Ed

Lord, C., Rutter, M., Goode, S., Heemsbergen, J., Jordan, H., Mawhood, L. and Schopler, E. (1989) 'Autism Diagnostic Observation Schedule (ADOS): A standardised observation of communicative and social behaviour'. *Journal of Autism and Developmental Disorders* 19, 185–212.

Lord, C., Rutter, M. and LeCouteur, A. (1994) 'Autism Diagnostic Interview – Revised (ADI): A revised version of a diagnostic interview for caregivers of individuals with possible pervasive developmental disorders'. *Journal of Autism and Developmental Disorders* 24, 659–85.

Rinaldi, W. (1996) *Understanding Ambiguity.* Windsor: NFER-Nelson.

Schopler, E., Reichler, R.J., Bashford, A. Lansing, M.D. and Marcus, L.M. (1990) *The Psycho-Educational Profile – Revised* (PEP-R). Austin, Texas: Pro-Ed.

Schopler, E., Reichler, R.J. and Rochen Renner, B. (2002) *The Childhood Autism Rating Scale* (CARS). (9th edn) Los Angeles: Western Psychological Services.

Wing, L. (1999) *Diagnostic Interview for Social and Communication Disorders* (DISCO). London: The National Autistic Society.

Materials for intervention

TEACCH
Treatment and Education of Autistic and related Communication Handicapped Children: University of North Carolina.
Website: www.teacch.com

PECS
Picture Exchange Communication System: Pyramid Educational Consultants UK Ltd., Pavilion House, 6–7 Old Steine, Brighton BN1 1EJ
Tel.: 0127 360 9555
Fax: 0127 360 9556
Website: www.pecs.org.uk

Computer-generated symbols (Boardmaker)
The Picture Communication Symbols © 1981, 2005 by Mayer-Johnson LLC. All Rights Reserved Worldwide. Used with permission.
Boardmaker is a trademark of Mayer-Johnson LLC.
Mayer-Johnson LLC, PO Box 1579, Solana Beach, CA 92075, USA
Tel.: (00 1) 858 550 0084
Fax: (00 1) 858 550 0449
Website: www.mayer-johnson.com
email: mayerj@mayer-johnson.com
(Also available from Speechmark Publishing)

A resource for computer-generated symbols
www.dotolearn.com

Circle of Friends
Mary Letheren Jones (1999)
Essex County Council Learning Services, PO Box 47,
County Hall, Chelmsford CM2 6WN

Social Stories
Carol Gray, Jenison Public Schools and Gray Center for
Social Learning and Understanding.
Website: www.thegraycenter.org

Gray, C. and Leigh White, A. (2002) *My Social Stories Book*. London: Jessica Kingsley.

Smith, C. (2003) *Writing and Developing Social Stories: Practical Interventions in Autism.* Bicester, Oxon: Speechmark.

Social skills programmes
Aarons, M and Gittens, T. (1998) *Autism: A Social Skills Approach for Children and Adolescents.* Bicester, Oxon: Speechmark.

Aarons, M. and Gittens, T. (2003) *Social Skills Programmes: An Integrated Approach from Early Years to Adolescence.* Bicester, Oxon: Speechmark.

Kelly, A. (various dates) (i) *Talkabout* (ii) *Talkabout Activities* (iii) *Talkabout Relationships.* Bicester, Oxon: Speechmark.

Emotional understanding
Mind Reading – The Interactive Guide to Emotions. CD-ROM and DVD produced by Human Emotions Ltd. and Cambridge University Autism Research Centre (2002). Published by Jessica Kingsley Publishers and enquiries regarding availability to the National Autistic Society.

School transitions
Maines, B. and Robinson, G. (1997) *The Big School* (4th edn) Bristol: Lucky Duck.

Glossary

ASD – autistic spectrum disorder

IEP – individual education plan/programme

LSA – learning support assistant (this role may also be referred to as the pupil's 1:1)

PECS – Picture Exchange Communication System: a pre-verbal communication schedule

TEACCH – Treatment and Education of Autistic and related Communication handicapped CHildren

SENCO – Special Educational Needs Coordinator

SLT – Speech and Language Therapist

TA – teaching assistant (this role may also be referred to as classroom assistant or nursery nurse (particularly in special education).